Selected Poems

LES A. MURRAY

Selected Poems

First published in 1986 by
Carcanet Press Limited
208-212 Corn Exchange Buildings
Manchester M4 3BQ

British Library Cataloguing in Publication Data
Murray, Les A.
  Selected Poems.
  I. Title
  821   PR6063.U74

  ISBN 0-85635-667-0

The Publisher acknowledges the financial assistance
of the Arts Council of Great Britain.

Typeset by Bryan Williamson, Swinton, Berwickshire
Printed in England by SRP Ltd., Exeter

Acknowledgements

This selection includes poems from *The Ilex Tree* (1965), *The Weatherboard Cathedral* (1969), *Poems Against Economics* (1972), *Lunch and Counter Lunch* (1974), *The Vernacular Republic* (1976 and 1982), *Ethnic Radio* (1979), and *The People's Otherworld* (1983). Additional poems, not previously published in book form, appeared in *Planet*, *PN Review*, *The Times Literary Supplement* and *Verse*.

Contents

Driving Through Sawmill Towns

1

In the high cool country,
having come from the clouds,
down a tilting road
into a distant valley,
you drive without haste. Your windscreen parts the forest,
swaying and glancing, and jammed midday brilliance
crouches in clearings...
then you come across them,
the sawmill towns, bare hamlets built of boards
with perhaps a store,
perhaps a bridge beyond
and a little sidelong creek alive with pebbles.

2

The mills are roofed with iron, have no walls:
you look straight in as you pass, see lithe men working,
the swerve of a winch,
dim dazzling blades advancing
through a trolley-borne trunk
till it sags apart
in a manifold sprawl of weatherboards and battens.

The men watch you pass:
when you stop your car and ask them for directions,
tall youths look away –
it is the older men who
come out in blue singlets and talk softly to you.

Beside each mill, smoke trickles out of mounds
of ash and sawdust.

You glide on through town,
your mudguards damp with cloud.
The houses there wear verandahs out of shyness,
all day in calendared kitchens, women listen
for cars on the road,
lost children in the bush,
a cry from the mill, a footstep –
nothing happens.

The half-heard radio sings
its song of sidewalks.

Sometimes a woman, sweeping her front step,
or a plain young wife at a tankstand fetching water
in a metal bucket will turn around and gaze
at the mountains in wonderment,
looking for a city.

Evenings are very quiet. All around
the forest is there.
As night comes down, the houses watch each other:
a light going out in a window here has meaning.

You speed away through the upland,
glare through towns
and are gone in the forest, glowing on far hills.

On summer nights
ground-crickets sing and pause.
In the dark of winter, tin roofs sough with rain,
downpipes chafe in the wind, agog with water.
Men sit after tea
by the stove while their wives talk, rolling a dead match
between their fingers,
thinking of the future.

The Burning Truck

It began at dawn with fighter planes:
they came in off the sea and didn't rise,
they leaped the sandbar one and one and one
coming so fast the crockery they shook down
off my kitchen shelves was spinning in the air
when they were gone.

They came in off the sea and drew a wave
of lagging cannon-shells across our roofs.
Windows spat glass, a truck took sudden fire,
out leaped the driver, but the truck ran on,
growing enormous, shambling by our street-doors,
coming and coming....

By every right in town, by every average
we knew of in the world, it had to stop,
fetched up against a building, fall to rubble
from pure force of burning, for its whole
body and substance were consumed with heat
but it would not stop.

And all of us who knew our place and prayers
clutched our verandah-rails and window-sills,
begging that truck between our teeth to halt,
keep going, vanish, strike...but set us free.
And then we saw the wild boys of the street
go running after it.

And as they followed, cheering, on it crept,
windshield melting now, canopy-frame a cage
torn by gorillas of flame, and it kept on
over the tramlines, past the church, on past
the last lit windows, and then out of the world
with its disciples.

An Absolutely Ordinary Rainbow

The word goes round Repins,
the murmur goes round Lorenzinis.
At Tattersalls, men look up from sheets of numbers,
the Stock Exchange scribblers forget the chalk in their hands
and men with bread in their pockets leave the Greek Club:
There's a fellow crying in Martin Place. They can't stop him.

The traffic in George Street is banked up for half a mile
and drained of motion. The crowds are edgy with talk
and more crowds come hurrying. Many run in the back streets
which minutes ago were busy main streets, pointing:
There's a fellow weeping down there. No one can stop him.

The man we surround, the man no one approaches
simply weeps, and does not cover it, weeps
not like a child, not like the wind, like a man
and does not declaim it, nor beat his breast, nor even
sob very loudly – yet the dignity of his weeping

holds us back from his space, the hollow he makes about him
in the midday light, in his pentagram of sorrow,
and uniforms back in the crowd who tried to seize him
stare out at him, and feel, with amazement, their minds
longing for tears as children for a rainbow.

Some will say, in the years to come, a halo
or force stood around him. There is no such thing.
Some will say they were shocked and would have stopped him
but they will not have been there. The fiercest manhood,
the toughest reserve, the slickest wit amongst us

trembles with silence, and burns with unexpected
judgements of peace. Some in the concourse scream
who thought themselves happy. Only the smallest children
and such as look out of Paradise come near him
and sit at his feet, with dogs and dusty pigeons.

Ridiculous, says a man near me, and stops
his mouth with his hands, as if it uttered vomit –
and I see a woman, shining, stretch her hand
and shake as she receives the gift of weeping;
as many as follow her also receive it

and many weep for sheer acceptance, and more
refuse to weep for fear of all acceptance,
but the weeping man, like the earth, requires nothing,
the man who weeps ignores us, and cries out
of his writhen face and ordinary body

not words, but grief, not messages, but sorrow
hard as the earth, sheer, present as the sea –
and when he stops, he simply walks between us
mopping his face with the dignity of one
man who has wept, and now has finished weeping.

Evading believers, he hurries off down Pitt Street.

Toward the Imminent Days
for Geoff and Sally Lehmann

1

Midmorning, September, and red tractors climb
on a landscape wide as all forgiveness. Clouds
in the west horizon, parrots twinkling down
on Leary's oats, on Stewarts' upturned field –

good friends are blood relations that you choose.
The phrase discovers me in the heart of farmland
harpstringing fences, coming back into my life.
A thick coin flips out of my mouth, I leap over thistles

and I think of your wedding, I make it shine among trees
in a vast evening cattlecamp lit by jewelled pendants, by plates,
by brass lamps suspended on trace chains at great height.
The beams of carlights conjure our bustling assembly.

Now the minister comes, with rapid changes of car,
and all of us, painters, centurions in mufti, horses,
lawyers discoursing on sheepback, all drink up quickly,
the hush of Queensland falling on sculptress and ghost.

As the words begin, your pledges rising, whole branches
of blossom appear on the tree your lives have reached,
from out of sight of land, an incredibly high
hymeneal piping makes my wineglass sing –

or so I choose to remember it in the country
and from that glass I'll drink your health always,
recalling your abundant house, the dancing,
your shovelled cake rich as the history of Calabria.

2

Topping ridges, considering some poor late gift
(my gifts this year are so very nearly ineffable)
I think of a day too great for the calendar numbers
that, faintest in winter, grows like a buried moon,

a radiant season swelling through the horizons
beyond September, mortality crumbling down
till on summer mornings, a farm boy can see through the hills,
the roots of pumpkin-vines knotting clean under New England.

With Advent so near beneath a man's pitchfork,
the wild and paddocks rising into each other
in the whole green crescent of the tented air,
to keep the dead at peace, wise farmers talk drought,

Hanrahan's comfort – but wheat is crowding through cities
Cabinet ministers pace in the light of Canowindra.
As cattle cross on the stockroutes, a commonwealth walking,
young men leap rivers and, lounging in grasses that threaten

the smaller brick towns, they long for a splendid alert.
Only marriage will save them. The hills are so riddled with fun
that timber dance-halls hide out in the ruins of whisky
and Holdens surging from under barns at midday

are buffed by almost uncontainable winds
for the woman of seed who is the landscape is seizing
all things in her gift. Verandahs sail home on the hills
till the imminent day is burned remote by the sun.

3

Singing All living are wild in the imminent days
I walk into furrows end-on and they rise through my flesh
burying worlds of me. It is the clumsiest dancing,
this walking skewways over worn-ocean that heaps

between skid and crumble with lumped stones in ambush for feet
but it marches with seed and steadiness, knowing the land.
As the dogs set out from the house, minute, black, running,
I am striding on over the fact that it is the earth

that holds our mark longest, that soil dug never returns
to primal coherence. Dead men in the fathoms of fields
sustain without effort millennial dark columns
and to their suspension, the crystal centuries come –

But now I am deep in butter-thick native broom
wading, sky-happy, a cotton-bright drover of bees.
As I break out of flowers, the dogs who have only
chaos for language, and territory dense in their fur

mob me, leaping, and I am too merry with farms
not to run with them, to trample my shadow on sticks:
outpacing dignity, I collide with sheer landscapes
dancing with dogs in the rain of information.

4

In my aunt's house, the milk jug's beaded crochet cover
tickles the ear. We've eaten boiled things with butter.
Pie spiced like islands, dissolving in cream, is now
dissolving in us. We've reached the teapot of calm.

The table we sit at is fashioned of three immense
beech boards out of England. The minute widths of the years
have been refined in the wood by daughters' daughters.
In the year of Nelson, I notice, the winter was mild.

But our talk is cattle and cricket. My quiet uncle
has spent the whole forenoon sailing a stump-ridden field
of blady-grass and Pleistocene clay never ploughed
since the world's beginning. The Georgic furrow lengthens

in ever more intimate country. But we're talking bails,
stray cattle, brands. In the village of Merchandise Creek
there's a post in a ruined blacksmith shop that bears
a charred-in black-letter script of iron characters,

hooks, bars, conjoined letters, a weird bush syllabary.
It is the language of property seared into skin
but descends beyond speech into the muscles of cattle,
the world of feed as it shimmers in cattle minds.

My uncle, nodding, identifies the owners
(I gather M-bar was mourned by thousands of head).
It has its roots in meadows deeper than Gaelic,
my uncle's knowledge. Farmers longest in heaven

share slyly with him in my aunt's grave mischievous smile
that shines out of every object in my sight
in these loved timber rooms at the threshold of grass.
The depth in this marriage will heal the twentieth century.

5

Broad afternoon. The hired boy and I
stack saccaline in the hammer-mill by the sheds
till the air is coarse with silage. Clouds of fowls
and black, shape-shifting turkeys frisk our output

But we are watching how my cousins flare
around the cowbails, yarding up fresh milkers,
knee-gripping buckets (strophe, antistrophe);
no primitive bush pumpkin eaters here,

these are prosperous, well-mannered children;
gentle with cows. Even the youngest's a dairyman
concerned with his poddy-calves. No one here will be
a visitor gnawed by lifelong celebration.

We look at them. Even the hired boy knows
at his age, that freedom is memory. He sees hope
in asking me about cities. How can I tell him
the cities are debris driven by explosions

whose regulation takes a merciless cunning?
I love my cities too well not to start at least there.
I turn his question away, out into the hills
where the bold rabbit-shooter may learn his life from a pool

or consider the turkeys (their splendour coherent with filth)
if they mistake your toes for corn, look out
my grandfather vomited once and our fowls got blind drunk –
I rack my past for a health the boy can use.

17

In the land of cows-to-milk
there was once a wobbly calf
and he grew to be a bull
scraping up armorial dirt
with a pedigree to bellow
in the bullness of his season
and we used to chase him home
whoa back bull!
Through our neighbours' flagrant fences
till my father linked a chain
round his horns to catch and lead:
You will save your herd-improvements
for our own herd, mister bull!
He was docile for a time
till he found he was the strong one
and began to trot – whoa bull!

Whoa bull – and the running started
as depicted in the friezes.
Loop his chain around a sapling
(wrench of splinters) try a tree!

Block him, yard him, bloody bull
I'll sell you for dogmeat, screamed
my short-legged father, clinging, swinging
on the chain and prancing faster
than the sons of man can run
skipping on the ringbarked hills
stumbling, leaping on the mountains
Jersey farmer, Jersey bull
raging under the horizons
until, sometime after dark,
soaked with tropic and Antarctic
spray and dust of Innamincka
in murderous mutual respect
man and bull would stagger home
linked, supporting one another

wheezing Corn, moaning Supper
shedding forests from their chain.

When you see him, ask my father.

7

Dog roses, wild clematis, indigo
crossing the creek on my mind's feet, though,
I walk on home where the stars are thinnest, glancing
back at the village with one human house

that is my uncle's farm. Nightjars fly through me,
snipping winged ants. Into the brimming hills
cattle graze beyond the human marriages,
and the one-globe kitchen windows, miles apart,

approach the quiet of boats far out on the year
whose wake is all that will persist of them.
What lasts is the voyage of families down their name.
Houses pass into paradise continually,

voices, loved fields, all wearing away into heaven.
As the cornplanter sings out to the rising month
bush-hidden creeks in the rabbit country wash
like a clear stone in my mind, the heavenly faculty.

Hiles' paddock leans on its three-strand fence in the dark
bending the road a little with its history.
Our lives are refined by remotest generations.
Months late, I catch up with your wedding once again,

the candles laughter chicken-legs speeches champagne
I pass with a wave (lifting a friend from the wheeltracks)
and full of a lasting complicity, old henchman,
about the life of this world, strike home over grass.

For your wedding, I wish you the frequent image of farms.

The Names of the Humble

Fence beyond fence from breakfast
I climb through into my thought
And watch the slowing of herds into natural measures.

Nose down for hours, ingesting grass, they breathe grass,
Trefoil, particles, out of the soft-focus earth
Dampened by nose-damp. They have breathed great plateaux to
    dust.

But a cow's mouth circling on feed, the steady radius
Shifting (dry sun) as she shifts
Subsumes, say, two thirds of mankind. Our cities, our circles.

They concede me a wide berth at first. I go on being harmless
And some graze closer, gradually. It is like watching
An emergence. Persons.

Where cattletracks mount
Boustrophedon to the hills
I want to discern the names of all the humble.

                    *

A meaningful lack in the mother-tongue of factories:
How do you say *one* cattle? Cow, bull, steer
But nothing like *bos*. Cattle is *chattel*, is owned

By man the castrator,
Body and innocence, cud and death-bellow and beef.
Bush people say *beast*, and mean no more fabulous creature

And indeed, from the moon to the alphabet, there aren't many.
Surely the most precious Phoenician cargo
Was that trussed rough-breathing ox turned dawnward to lead

All Europe's journey.

                    *

20

Far back as I can glimpse with descendant sight
Beyond roads or the stave-plough, there is a boy on cold upland,
Gentle tapper of veins, a blood-porridge eater,
His ringlets new-dressed with dung, a spear in his fist,

It is thousands of moons to the cattle-raid of Cooley

But we could still find common knowledge, verb-roots
And noun-bark enough for an evening fire of sharing
Cattle-wisdom,

Though it is a great year yet
Till Prithū will milk from the goddess (*O rich in cheer, come!*)
And down though his fingers into the rimmed vessel earth

Grain and food-gardens.
We are entirely before
The seed-eater towns.

*

A sherry-eyed Jersey looks at me. Fragments of thoughts
That will not ripple together worry her head

It is sophistication trying to happen

There's been betrayal enough, and eons enough.
Or no more than focus, then,
Trying to come up as far as her pupils.

Her calm gifts all central,
Her forehead a spiked shield to wolves
She bobs in her hull-down affinities.

The knotted sway pole along which her big organs hang
(It will offer them ruthlessly downward when knob joints cave in)
Rests unafraid in enzyme courtesies, though,

Steadier than cognitions speckling brains.

Since I've sunk my presence into the law
That every beast shall be apportioned space
According to display, I unfurl a hand.

She dribbles, informing
Her own weighted antique success
And stays to pump the simpler, infinite herbage.

*

Her Normandy bones
The nap of her Charolais colour

The ticks on her elder are such
Muscatels of good blood.

If I envy her one thing
It is her ease with this epoch.
A wagtail switching left-right, left-right on her rump.

Where cattletracks climb
Rice-terrace-wise to the hills
I want to speak the names of all the humble.

Boöpis

Coming out of reflections
I find myself in the earth.
                    My cow going on
into the creek from this paspalum-thatched tunnel-track
divides her hoofs among the water's impediments,
clastic and ungulate stones.
                    She is just deep
enough to be suckling the stream when she drinks from it.

22

Wetted hoofs, like hers,
incised in the alluvium
this grave's-width ramp up through the shoulder of the bank
but cattle paunches with their tongue-mapped girths also
brushed in glazes,
easements and ample places
at the far side of things from subtractive plating of spades
or the vertical silvers a coffin will score, sinking.

North, the heaped districts, and south
there'd be at least a Pharaoh's destruction of water
suspended above me in this chthonic section.
Seeds fall in here from the poise
of ploughland, grass land.
                                    I could be easily
foreclosed to a motionless size in the ruins of gloss.

The old dead, though, are absorbed, becoming strata.
The crystals, too, of glaze or matt, who have
not much say in a slump
seem coolly balanced toward me.

                              At this depth among roots
I thank God's own sacrifice
that I am not here with seeds and a weighty request
from the upper fields,
my own words constrained with a cord.
Not being that way, if I met the lady of summer,
the beautiful cow-eyed one, I would be saying:

Madam, the children of the overworld
cannot lay down their instruments at will.
Babel in orbit maps the hasty parks,
missile and daisy scorn the steady husbands
and my countrymen mix green with foreign fruit

but Minotaur has no faith to keep, wronged Lady.

József

M.J.K. 1883-1974 in piam memoriam

You ride on the world-horse once
no matter how brave your seat
or polished your boots, it may gallop you
into undreamed-of fields

but this field's outlandish: Australia!
To end in this burnt-smelling, blue-hearted
metropolis of sore feet and trains
(though the laughing bird's a good fellow).

Outlandish not to have died
in king-and-kaiserly service
dismounted, beneath the smashed guns
or later, with barons and credit

after cognac, a clean pistol death.
Alas, a small target, this heart.
Both holes were in front, though, entry
and exit. I learned to relish that.

Strange not to have died with the Kingdom
when Horthy's fleet sank, and the betting
grew feverish, on black and on red,
to have outlived even my Friday club

and our joke: *senilis senili*
gaudet. I bring home coffee now.
Dear God, not one cafe in this place,
no Andrássy-street, no Margaret's Island...

no law worth the name: they are British
and hangmen and precedent-quibblers
make rough jurisprudence at best.
Fairness, of course; that was their word.

24

I don't think Nature speaks English.
I used to believe I knew enough
with *gentleman, whisky, handicap*
and perhaps *tweed*. French lacked all those.

I learned the fine detail at seventy
out here. Ghosts in many casinos
must have smiled as I hawked playing cards
to shady clubs up long stairways

and was naturalized by a Lord Mayor
and many bookmakers, becoming a
New Australian. My son claims he always
was one. We had baptized him Gino

in Hungary. His children are natives
remote as next century. My eyes
are losing all faces, all letters,
the colours go, red, white, now green

into Hungary, Hungary of the poplar trees
and the wide summers where I am young
in uniform, riding with Nelly,
the horseshoes' noise cupping our speeches.

I, Mórelli József Károly,
once attorney, twice gunshot, thrice rich,
my cigarettes, monogrammed, from Kyriazi
once married (dear girl!) to a Jew

(gaining little from that but good memories
though my son's uniforms fitted her son
until it was next year in Cape Town)
am no longer easy to soften.

I will eat stuffed peppers and birds' milk,
avoid nuns, who are monstrous bad luck,
write letters from memory, smoke Winstons
and flex my right elbow at death

and, more gently, at living.

The Breach

I am a policeman
it is easier to make me seem an oaf
than to handle the truth

I came from a coaldust town
when I was seventeen, because there was nothing
for a young fellow there

the Force drew me because of a sense I had
and have grown out of

I said to Ware once, Harry, you're the best
cop of the lot: you only arrest falls
he was amused

I seem to be making an inventory of my life
but in that house opposite, first floor
there is a breach
and me, in this body I am careful with,
I'm going to have to enter that house soon

and stop that breach

it is a bad one people could fall through
we know that three have
and he's got a child poised

I have struck men in back rooms late at night
with faces you could fall a thousand feet down
and I've seen things in bowls

the trick is not to be a breach yourself
and to stop your side from being one
I suppose

the sniper Spiteri, when I was just out of cadets –
some far-west cockies' boys straight off the sheep train
came up with their .303s and offered to help
they were sixteen years old

we chased them away, not doubting for a minute
they could do what they said
bury your silver the day we let that start

now I've said my ideals

Snowy cut, snow he cut...
A razor-gang hood my uncle claims he met
is running through my mind
in Woolloomooloo, wet streets, the nineteen twenties
dear kind Snowy Cutmore

Snowy cuts no more
he was a real breach

also, in our town, I
remember the old hand bowsers, that gentle apop-
poplexy of benzine in the big glass heads

twenty years since I saw them

There's a moment with every man who has started a stir

when he tires of it, wants to put it aside
and be back, unguilty, that morning, pouring the milk

that is the time to separate him from it
if I am very good I'll judge that time
just about right

the ideal is to keep the man and stop
the breach
that's the high standard

but the breach must close

if later goes all right
I am going to paint the roof of our house
on my day off.

Aqualung Shinto
for Chris Koch

All day above the Japanese fleet,
the zenith sun between the islands
unmoving. We were after the flagship

and kept diving, finding tackle
jettisoned in her agony. My
shadow over the sand floor curved

on chain, on wavering metal forms,
Don saying *Be careful of any ammo,*
it could still give us the instant bends.

We were following the logic
of a dying ship among islands: here
he would have considered beaching her, here
the sub may have come for the admiral. We dived

in lucid water, tracing down
the death-hours of an Imperial captain
thirty years wiser than we were

in settling steel, in shouting men
in – reached after final avalanche cruising –
a peaceful Sun, that shapelessness.

We would come up from the dreamlight plane
and eat meals aboard the boat
Where we want her to lie, I guess

is a place neither dry nor drowned
where we could drift in Dante-style
and observe grotesques of courage

performed by knights of bushido in
tight black jackets. Quintessence movies.
I finished my can. *I would go up*

to Yamada and address him: Captain
I was born in 'thirty-eight
please give me what you own of me.

Those days, below in the sharks' kingdom
I kept remembering the iron ore ports
the black ships feeding at all times

and ore dust the colour of dried blood
on every object. Baseball Maru,
have you jettisoned anything

but the sword-wearers? That direct style?
(OVERACHIEVERS ARE JAPANESE
I wrote in pentel ink on the bulkhead.)

The water was layered like a pearl
clear-opaque-clear as I swam down
thinking of Marines twenty years in hiding
in dugouts, eating tadpole mush,
waiting to fight, treasuring a mortar

young men approaching fifty still
begging pardon, not having flown winged bombs

NIHON, the ultimate taut ship...

It shamed our carefully dazzle-painted
sanity. Don below me bubbled.
We were close to the flagship now
by the debris. Her presence was

longing for form. Her own. Again.
Aloud in my head I told myself
she would rise if I clapped my hands:

Towering superstructure, respectable
maritime-power lines – all just
askew by a fraction from machine history

in that copyist's deadness which betrays
cherishment of carp flags and tea brushes

design like poems in a culture-language.

At night, weighing the heart of it:
We are as easy to recruit
as ever, Don said,
but harder to command.

We are almost free of the State
almost clear, again, of armies.
It is time to oppress the State.

I think that is the history
of the rest of this century: cavaliers.
Were you romantic about cavaliers?

In the end it may be safer.
Defaming the high words – honour, courage –
has not stopped us. It has made us mad

we are maddened by a dumb spirit.
I lay there also musing. Waves.
Mishima died. Screams from Lod airport...

In the one entirely native
and wisest Japanese faith, I said,
a mirror hangs before sanctuaries.

Oh Zen makes colonials of a few
but each people has its proper Shinto
distinctive as verandah beams

hard to join as a stranger's childhood.
What withers us is that Australia
is a land of shamefaced shrines.

Perhaps, I went on, *the history coming*
is just more peoples passing for white,
fronting for themselves in English

and preserving their life in a closing fraction
from which leap unbelievably savage
flames. Which was your major point.

Imminent below us those nights, big
as an undersea ridge between the islands
a battleship of the Kongo class

was sending out her crew like waves:
Your fathers killed us, their minds aloof
from us in war as in any peace

and we were bringing pine-needle cakes, fox stories.

Their Cities, Their Universities

The men of my family danced a reel with sugar
        for two generations.
Robbie Burns was involved, that barley spirit
and history, and their fathers' voyage out
        but that is a novel.
The past explains us and it gets our flesh.

You would find most older Murray houses
        girt in some glitter
of bottle-glass in the paddocks, rum necks and whisky ghosts,
Wolfe's dark Aromatic Schnapps mostly grassroots-under now
        and insulin, insulin
as if to help the earth digest such crystals,
the thousand year jag, the gullies of downtrodden light.

31

It was in these spirits
that Veitch rode the frisky stick horse: *Go in, Mrs Maurer!*
        he's shying at ye!
and Sam towed Reggie-Boy shrieking behind his big Dodge
        in the splintering sulky.

It was through these that Hughie tumbled off his mare
        on the heirloom fiddle
and uncle Jock Clark danced Whee! in the shopping-day street
        prick burst from his trousers
asperging the people, a boneless arm limber as Jock
        and Burns got misquoted.

O

From the photograph, they look at me. Intelligent book-shy faces.
The scrolls of their fiddles curl at me, the pipe smoke goes up
fuzzy as the toddler who moved, or the man who shook his
        head at a fly
and smeared his last chance at history. The day is a bright one,

the golden wedding of Bella and John Allan,
old Bunyah Johnnie, seated here past the end
of his fabulous hospitality: *small table at Murrays*
today. Only twenty-six, not counting family –
That homestead is long gone – *man should hae led trumps –*
and the times are flattening down. The ringbarked Twenties.

        My great-grandfather John
is remembering what it is to conquer country:
        brush soil upturned,
thin-legged black people who would show you fruit,
a house set fair to a track to capture company.

Isabella, shrunken in silks, is holding minds with him
        (they are first cousins)
Gey strange it is, my hands free all day long now
of flour, milk, feathers. We never had to stint.
        Thank God for that, John.

32

John Murray of Bunyah, born in a Biscay storm
                my offshore Basque
                and thriftless as Montrose.

                              O

The drinking Murrays. They were rarely brutal.
It wasn't Murrays who rode the policeman with spurs
or gelded the half-witted youth to spare him problems
                but trotting through town
whips coiled and pipes alight, drawing revellers to them
and holding forth on music and seeds and the wurrld
                in their fathers' accent
and going home after for three nights, cooeeing abstemious
settlers from bed to hooting strathspey contests
and holding Saturday dances from Thursday night on
with their children milking a hundred cows in jig time
and schottische time, as the fiddlers raised the sun,
                that was the notion.

                After the heights
Grandfather, crossed, would upend the breakfast table
                and then his breakfast:
Father's sick. Walk quiet. He'll draw the whip on you.
He has been out of Sense and Worth in timber rooms
where men make bets and spittle beads, whooping their Lallans,
the night-sugar world where Burns is an evil spirit
                and self a form of anger.

                              O

Aunts with a nose for sin, young chaps with haircuts
combed like an open ginger book, pretty girls like a leafed one
relax from their poses, stroll off into marriages, deaths.

                Here at the focus
the sun goes under the paddocks, though, and pipers
are bulging the house with their summoned howling tune
and the drinkers, the brothers, candles in their hands

are kneeling on the floor to judge the tramping beat
        and the style of it:
            The big bloke's stepping fine!

And Veitch is confiding the hard drink to get into
a man is the second one. He means, for subversion.
        Veitch's shield against
inspectors, collectors, police is a happy day
that leaves them sitting about, hiccuping and ashamed
or lurching from their cars miles off, ashamed, hiccuping.

Wives and sisters are forbidden the shamanism of glass;
            they go busy, or proud
or brandish the Word, that soured woman's weapon
cold-hammered by Knox, fresh honed by the Wee Free Kirk,
        hard splinter of that Faith
        which overcame religion,

but the patriarchs are keeping their own time
like a door in the farm-dull days, and separate as logic.
        Boys nodding in cars outside
the pubs work promised ground they will not inherit.
It distils too sweet. Though it is all their wages.
They hear their lives going wheedle-and-away
on the four strained wires of a fiddle, in a spent tradition
Good on ye, Allan! and singing with no terms.
Scotland is a place Dad goes when he drinks rum
        but their feet are tapping.

They wasted their lands for that (and for all that)
        the redhaired Murrays.
The reasons are a novel, incomplete as cultures
now everywhere become. It is almost overt now:

            we are going to the cause
            not coming from it.

Kiss of the Whip

In Cardiff, off Saint Mary's Street
there in the porn shops you could get
a magazine called Kiss of the Whip.
I used to pretend I'd had poems in it.

Kiss of the Whip. I never saw it.
I might have encountered familiar skills
having been raised in a stockwhip culture.
Grandfather could dock a black snake's head,

Stanley would crack the snake for preference
leap from his horse grab whirl and jolt!
the popped head hummed from his one-shot slingshot.
The whips themselves were black, fine-braided

arm-coiling beasts that could suddenly flourish
and cut a cannibal strip from a bull
(millisecond returns) or idly behead an
ant on the track. My father did that.

A knot in the lash would kill a rabbit.
There were decencies: good dogs and children
were flogged with the same lash doubled back.
A horsehair plait on the tip for a cracker

sharpened the note. For ten or twelve thousand
years this was the sonic barrier's
one human fracture. Whip-cracking is that:
thonged lightning making the leanest thunder.

When black snakes go to Hell they are
affixed by their fangs to carved whip-handles
and fed on nothing but noonday heat,
sweat and flowing rumps and language.

They writhe up dust-storms for revenge
and send them roaring where creature comfort's
got with a touch of the lash. And that
is a temple yard that will bear more cleansing

before, through droughts and barracks, those
lax, quiet-speaking, sudden fellows
emerge where skill unbraids from death
and mastering, in Saint Mary's Street.

Portrait of the Autist as a New World Driver

A car is also
a high-speed hermitage. Here
only the souls of policemen can get at you.
Who would put in a telephone,
that merciless foot-in-the-door
of realities, realties?

Delight of a stick-shift –
farms were abandoned for these pleasures. Second
to third in this Mazda is a stepped inflection
third back to first at the lights
a concessive
V of junction.

Under the overcoming
undiminishing sky you are scarcely supervised:
you can let out language
to exercise, to romp in the grass beyond Greek.
You can rejoice in tongues,
orotate parafundities.

They simplify
who say the Artist's a child
they miss the point closely: an artist
even if he has brothers, sisters, spouse
is an only child.

Among the self-taught
the loners, chart-freaks, bush-encyclopedists
there are protocols, too: we meet
gravely as stiff princes, and swap fact:
did you know some bats can climb side on?

Mind you, Hitler was one of us.
He had a theory. We also count stern scholars
in whose disputes you almost hear the teenage
hobbyist still disputing proof and mint
and wheelmen who murmur *Suffering is bourgeois.*

But swapping cogs to pass a
mountainous rig and its prime mover, I
reflect that driving's a mastery the mastered
are holding on to.
It has gone down among the ancient crafts
to hide in our muscles.

Indeed, if you asked
where the New World is, I'd have to answer
he is in his car
he is booming down the highways
in that funnel of blue-green-gold, tree-flecked and streaming
light that a car is always breaking out of –

We didn't come of
the New World, but we've owned it.
From a steady bang, ever more globes, flying outward;
strange tunings are between us.
Of course we love our shells: they make the anthill
bearable. Of course the price is blood.

Sidere Mens Eadem Mutato
a spiral of sonnets for Robert Ellis

Out of the Fifties, a time of picking your nose
while standing at attention in civilian clothes
we travelled luxury class in our drift to the city
not having a war, we went to university.
We learned to drink wine, to watch Swedish movies, and pass
as members, or members-in-law, of the middle class
but not in those first days when, stodge-fed, repressed,
curfewed and resented, we were the landladies' harvest.
I had meant to write a stiff poem about that, to be
entitled NOTES FROM THE HOUSE OF MRS HARVEY
it might have been unkind, in parts – but then, to be honest
one did evict me for eating my dessert first
and even from the kindliest, we were
estranged, as from parents, in a green Verona

O

a nail-biting fiefdom of suede boots, concupiscence, tea,
a garden pruned by the *Herald* angels yearly.
In that supermarket of styles, with many a setback
we tried everything on, from Law School Augustan to rat pack
and though in Chinese my progress was smooth up to *K'ung*
and in German I mastered the words that follow *Achtung*
in my slow-cycling mind an eloquence not yet articulate
was trying to say Youth. This. I will take it straight.
And you were losing your bush millenarian faith – I
remember your dread of the Wrath on first tasting coffee.
We were reading Fisher Library, addressing gargoyles on the stair,
drafting self after self on Spir-O-Bind notepaper
as the tidal freshers poured in, with hard things to learn
in increasing droves they were getting off at Redfern.

Literate Australia was British, or babu at least,
before Vietnam and the American conquest
career had overwhelmed learning most deeply back then:

a major in English made one a minor Englishman
and woe betide those who stepped off the duckboards of that.
Slacking and depth were a single morass. But a spirit
of unresolved life caught more and more in its powerful
field. It slowed their life to bulk wine and pool.
Signals had to be found. The day you gave up fornication
we took your WetChex and, by insufflation,
made fat balloons of them, to glisten aloft in the sun
above the Quad, the Great Hall, the Carillion –
and that was Day One in the decade of chickens-come-home
that day kids began smoking the armpit hairs of wisdom.

O

It is some while since we roomed at Bondi Beach
and heard the beltmen crying each to each.
Good friends we made while snatching culture between
the cogs of the System (they turned slower then)
reemerge, and improve as their outlines grow more clear
(but where's Lesley now? and Jacqueline, what of her?)
Academe has grown edgier. Many still drowse in the sun
but *intellect* sounds like the cocking of a sten gun.
Remember urbanity, by which our time meant
allusion to little-known Names in a special accent?
It persists – but war's grown; war, snarling out of that trip
in which Freud and Marx are left and right thongs in a goosestep.
Mind you, Jane Fonda plays in it too. It's fairly thin war.
The tiger is real, and in pain. He is fed on paper.

When the decorous towers were shaken by screams and bare
        hands
they deserved to be shaken. They had sought to classify humans.
The kids were constructing a poem of feathers and pain,
a prayer, a list, a shriek, it reached no resolution
except to stay crucial. Their prophets said different things:
Pour wax on the earth. Beat spirals into rings.
But though they shamed Magog their father and crippled his war
their own gnawed at them. They colonized one another.

With the cameras running, somehow the beat had to go on
(in times of trend, death comes by relegation)
but selfhood kept claiming the best people hand over fist
in a few months a third of mankind had been called fascist –
as the music slowed, the big track proved to be
"Fantasia of the World as a Softened University".

O

Some things did change. Middle class girls learned to swear
men walked on the face of the moon once the Pill had tamed her
and we entered our thirties. No protest avails against that
the horror of Time is, people don't snap out of it.
Now student politicoes well known in our day
have grown their hair two inches and are running the country.
Revolution's established. There will soon be degrees
conferred, with fistshake and speech, by the Dean of Eumenides.
The degree we attained was that brilliant refraction of will
that leaves one in several minds when facing evil.
It's still being offered. The Church of Jesus and Newman
did keep some of us balanced concerning the meanings of "human"
that greased golden term (all the rage in the new demiurgy)
though each new Jerusalem tempts the weaker clergy.

O

Academe has gained ground. She is the great house of our age,
replacing Society, granting the entree to privilege
likewise a museum, of peoples, of scholars, of writing –
vampires at times may tend an iron lung.
Her study is fashion, successive lock-gates leaking Time
she loves this new goddess for whom abortion is orgasm,
the talkative one. Nothing, now, less intense
could thrill an elite above unwilled experience.
When our elders, the castes who live by delegation,
turned in, like unlicensed guns, imagination,
thought, spirit, ideals to the all-wise University
there were aspects of learning they did not foresee
like being the Masses, Funny Little Men
who live in the Suburbs and resemble Eichmann.

O

Academe is the class struggle, and whatever side
prevails will be hers. But I'm no alma-matricide
her task's also central: not making chemists and lawyers
but getting the passionate through their mating-and-war-years
to compromise. Remember? These shibboleths seem very real
in the light of a burning green stick. But where death's not literal
grace must be discerning. We have seen noble minds become
     rabid
and, as democrats, treat the Union stewards like dirt –
doctrine takes such a long view, especially in colonies
that I'm grateful, like you, for downtown and country-town eyes
that glint and stay subtle while knowledge is power and foreign
through these, and some clowning, we master generalization
the blade of Caesarean rebirth which, day after day,
freed words in us. And cut our homes away.

O

That's the nub and the cork of it. Most rhymes in -ism and -ation
are nothing but cabals, though, out to take over the nation
compared with true persons: with Peter who sought gallant war,
with Herr Doktor Kurt H., who was a Siegfried-figure
by his own admission, with Vanessa Max Laurence Penny
of *Honi Soit* then – they were our peerless company –
with Duncan the Sydney historian who in an Australian course might send off the First Fleet by August:
and Dave Croll who died of a train, having seen much reality
these dine with my uncles and hills in the restaurant of memory
(which is also a starship, a marriage, a crystal of heaven)
with the droll men of Physics who one day would capture the
     Quark
with Germaine a few tables off winning a hard conversation
and Lex who cried *Poetry is not the wine but the cognac...*

The Broad Bean Sermon

Beanstalks, in any breeze, are a slack church parade
without belief, saying *trespass against us* in unison,
recruits in mint Air Force dacron, with unbuttoned leaves.

Upright with water like men, square in stem-section
they grow to great lengths, drink rain, keel over all ways,
kink down and grow up afresh, with proffered new greenstuff.

Above the cat-and-mouse floor of a thin bean forest
snails hang rapt in their food, ants hurry through several
      dimensions:
spiders tense and sag like little black flags in their cordage.

Going out to pick beans with the sun high as fence-tops, you
      find
plenty, and fetch them. An hour or a cloud later
you find shirtfulls more. At every hour of daylight

appear more that you missed: ripe, knobbly ones, fleshy-sided,
thin-straight, thin-crescent, frown-shaped, bird-shouldered,
      boat-keeled ones,
beans knuckled and single-bulged, minute green dolphins at
      suck,

beans upright like lecturing, outstretched like blessing fingers
in the incident light, and more still, oblique to your notice
that the noon glare or cloud-light or afternoon slants will uncover

till you ask yourself Could I have overlooked so many, or
do they form in an hour? unfolding into reality
like templates for subtly broad grins, like unique caught
      expressions,

like edible meanings, each sealed around with a string
and affixed to its moment, an unceasing colloquial assembly,
the portly, the stiff, and those lolling in pointed green slippers....

Wondering who'll take the spare bagfulls, you grin with happiness
– it is your health – you vow to pick them all
even the last few, weeks off yet, misshapen as toes.

The Action

We have spoken of the Action,
the believer in death, maker of tests and failures.
It is through the Action
that the quiet homes empty, and barrack beds fill up, and cities
that are cover from God.
The Action, continual breakthrough,
cannot abide slow speech. It invented Yokels,
it invented the Proles, who are difficult/noble/raffish,
it invented, in short, brave Us and the awful Others.
The smiling Action
makes all things new: its rites are father-killing,
sketching of pyramid plans, and the dance of Circles.

Turning slowly under trees, footing off the river's linen
to come into shade – some waterhens were subtly
edging away to their kampongs of chomped reeds –
eel-thoughts unwound through me. At a little distance
I heard New Year children slap the causeway.

                                                    Floating
in Coolongolook River, there below the junction
of Curreeki Creek,

                        water of the farms upheld me.

We were made by the Action:
the apes who agreed to speech ate those who didn't,
Action people tell us.
Rome of the waterpipes came of the Action, lost it,
and Louis' Versailles, in memory of which we mow grass.
Napoleon and Stalin were, mightily, the Action.
All the Civilizations, so good at royal arts and war
and postal networks –

it is the myriad Action
keeps them successive, prevents the achievement for good
of civilization.

Wash water, cattle water, irrigation-pipe-tang water
and water of the Kyle,
                    the chain-saw forests up there
where the cedar getter walks at night with dangling pockets,
water of the fern-tree gushers' heaping iron,
water of the bloodwoods, water of the Curreeki gold rush,
water of the underbrush sleeping shifts of birds
all sustained me,
                    thankful for great dinners
that had made me a lazy swimmer, marvellous floater,
looking up through oaks
                    to the mountain Coolongolook,
the increase-place of flying fox people, dancers –

Now talk is around of a loosening in republics,
retrievals of subtle water: all the peoples
who call themselves The People,
all the unnoticed cultures,
remnants defined by a tilt in their speech, traditions
that call the stars, say, Great Bluff, Five Hounds of Oscar,
the High and Low Lazies,
spells, moon-phase farming – all these are being canvassed.
The time has come round for republics of the cultures
and for rituals, with sound: the painful washings-clean
of smallpox blankets.
It may save the world,
or be the new Action.

                                        Leaves
were coming to my lips, and the picnic on the bank
made delicious smoke.
                    Soon, perhaps, I'd be ready
to go and eat steak amongst Grandmother's people,
talk even to children,
                    dipping my face again
I kneaded my muscles, softening the Action.

The Mitchells

I am seeing this: two men are sitting on a pole
they have dug a hole for and will, after dinner, raise
I think for wires. Water boils in a prune tin.
Bees hum their shift in unthinning mists of white

bursaria blossom, under the noon of wattles.
The men eat big meat sandwiches out of a styrofoam
box with a handle. One is overheard saying:
drought that year. Yes. Like trying to farm the road.

The first man, if asked, would say *I'm one of the Mitchells.*
The other would gaze for a while, dried leaves in his palm,
and looking up, with pain and subtle amusement,

say *I'm one of the Mitchells.* Of the pair, one has been rich
but never stopped wearing his oil-stained felt hat. Nearly every-
    thing
they say is ritual. Sometimes the scene is an avenue.

The Powerline Incarnation

When I ran to snatch the wires off our roof
hands bloomed teeth shouted I was almost seized
held back from this life
                    O flumes   O chariot reins
you cover me with lurids deck me with gaudies feed
my coronal   a scream sings in the air
above our dance   you slam it to me with farms
that you dark on and off numb hideous strong friend
Tooma and Geehi freak and burr through me
rocks fire-trails damwalls mountain-ash trees slew
to darkness through me   I zap them underfoot
with the swords of my shoes
                    I am receiving mountains
piloting around me Crackenback   Anembo

the Fiery Walls   I make a hit in towns
I've never visited: smoke curls lightbulbs pop grey
discs hitch and slow   I plough the face of Mozart
and Johnny Cash   I bury and smooth their song
I crack it for copper links and fusebox spiders
I call my Friend from the circuitry of mixers
whipping cream for a birthday I distract the immortal
Inhuman from hospitals
                              to sustain my jazz
and here is Rigel in a glove of flesh
my starry hand discloses smoke, cold Angel.

Vehicles that run on death come howling into
our street with lights a thousandth of my blue
arms keep my wife from my beauty   from my species
the jewel in my tips
                              I would accept her in
blind white remarriage   cover her with wealth
to arrest the heart   we'd share Apache leaps
crying out *Disyzygy!*
                              shield her from me, humans
from this happiness I burn to share   this touch
sheet car   live ladder   wildfire garden shrub –
away off I hear the bombshell breakers thrown
diminishing me   a meaninglessness coming
over the circuits
                    the god's deserting me
but I have dived in the mainstream   jumped the graphs
I have transited the dreams of crew-cut boys named Buzz
and the hardening music
                              to the big bare place
where the strapped-down seekers, staining white clothes,
come to be shown the Zeitgeist   passion and death my skin

my heart all logic   I am starring there
and must soon flame out
                              having seen the present god
It who feels nothing   It who answers prayers.

The Returnees

As we were rowing to the lakes
our oars were blunt and steady wings

the tanbark-coloured water was
a gruel of pollen: more coming down
hinted strange futures to our cells

the far hills ancient under it
the corn flats black-green under heat
were cut in an antique grainy gold

it was the light of Boeotian art.

O

Bestowing tourbillons that drowned
the dusty light we had used up
pulling the distance to us, we
were conscious of a lifelong sound

on everything, that low fly-humming
melismatic untedious endless
note that a drone-pipe-plus-chants or

(shielding our eyes, rocking the river)

a ballad – some ballads – catch, the one
some paintings and many yarners summon
the ground-note here of unsnubbing art

cicadas were in it, and that Gothic
towering of crystals in the trees
Jock Neilson cutting a distant log

O

still hearing, we saw a snake ahead
winding, being his own schnorkel

aslant in the swimming highlights, only
his head betrayed him, leading two
ripples and a scaled-down swirl. We edged

closer, were defied and breathed at.
A migrant, perhaps? a pioneer?
or had a kookaburra dropped

him, missing the organ-busting ground
and even the flat of the drinking-ground?

O

Touching the oars and riding, we
kept up with the blunt, heat-tasting head
debating its life, and sparing it

which is the good of Athens. Where
the rotted milk-wharf took the sun
flint-hard on top, dappling below

(remembered children danced up there
spinning their partners, the bright steel cans
a way of life. But a way of life.)

the snake rose like a Viking ship
signed mud with a scattering flourish and
was into the wale of potato ground

like a whip withdrawn. We punted off.

O

Oar-leather jumping in spaced kicks
against the swivel-screw of rowlocks
we hauled the slow bush headlands near

drinking beer, and talking a bit

such friendliness shone into us, such
dry complex cheer, insouciant calm

out of everything, the brain-shaped trees
the wrinkling middle-gleam, the still
indifferently well-wooded hills, it was

like rowing to meet your very best
passionately casual and dead friends
and feast with them on a little island

or an angel leaning down to one
queuing on the Day, to ask
what was the best throw that you did?

that note, raised to the pitch of tears:
tower of joking, star of skill,
gate of sardonyx and worn gold

*Black men and Rosenberg and I
have beliefs in common*, I exclaimed

and you were agreeing that Mao Tse-tung
had somehow come to Dunsinane –

O

any more heightening and it would
have been a test, but the centre we
had stirred stopped down again, one notch

to happiness, and we were let dip
our points in the wide stopped water and
reclaim our motion. Bloodwood trees

round there were in such a froth of bloom
their honey dripped on shale and gummed
blady-grass in wigwams and ant-towns

sweetness, infusing, followed us
Reality is somebody's, you said
with a new and wryly balanced smile

We're country, and Western, I replied.

Creeper Habit

On Bennelong Point
a two-dimensional tree
drapes the rock cutting.

Bird-flecked, self-espaliered
it issues out of the kerb
feeding on dead sparks
of the old tram depot;

a fig, its muscles
of stiffened chewing gum grip
the flutings and beads
of the crowbar-and-dynamite wall.

The tree has height and extent
but no roundness. Cramponned in cracks
its branches twine and utter
coated leaves.

With half its sky blank rock
it has little choice.
It has climbed high from a tiny sour gall

and spreads where it can,
feeding its leaves on the light
of North Shore windows.

Employment for the Castes in Abeyance

I was a translator at the Institute:
fair pay, clean work, and a bowerbird's delight
of theory and fact to keep the forebrain supple.

I was Western Europe. *Beiträge, reviste,
dissertaties, rapports,* turned English under my
one-fingered touch. Teacup-and-Remington days.

It was a job like Australia: peace and cover,
a recourse for exiles, poets, decent spies,
for plotters who meant to rise from the dead with their circle.

I was getting over a patch of free-form living:
flat food round the midriff, long food up your sleeves –
castes in abeyance, we exchanged these stories.

My Chekhovian colleague who worked as if under surveillance
would tell me tales of real life in Peking and Shanghai
and swear at the genders subsumed in an equation.

The trade was uneasy about computers, back then:
if they could be taught not to render, say, *out of sight
out of mind* as *invisible lunatic*

they might supersede us – not
because they'd be better. More on principle.
Not that our researchers were unkindly folk:

one man on exchange from Akademgorod
told me about earth's crustal plates, their ponderous
inevitable motion, collisions that raised mountain chains,

the continents rode on these Marxian turtles, it seemed;
another had brought slow death to a billion rabbits,
a third man had bottled the essence of rain on dry ground.

They were translators, too, our scientists:
they were translating the universe into science,
believing that otherwise it had no meaning.

Leaving there, I kept my Larousse and my Leutseligkeit
and I heard that machine translation never happened:
language defeated it. We are a language species.

I gather this provoked a shift in science,
that having become a side, it then changed sides
and having collapsed, continued at full tempo.

Prince Obolensky succeeded me for a time
but he soon returned to Fiji to teach Hebrew.
In the midst of life, we are in employment:

seek, travel and print, seek-left-right-travel-and-bang
as the Chinese typewriter went which I saw working
when I was a translator in the Institute.

The Buladelah-Taree Holiday Song Cycle

1

The people are eating dinner in that country north of Legge's
    Lake;
behind flywire and venetians, in the dimmed cool, town people
    eat Lunch.

Plying knives and forks with a peek-in sound, with a tuck-in
    sound
they are thinking about relatives and inventory, they are talking
    about customers and visitors.
In the country of memorial iron, on the creek-facing hills there,
they are thinking about bean plants, and rings of tank water, of
    growing a pumpkin by Christmas;
rolling a cigarette, they say thoughtfully Yes, and their companion
    nods, considering.
Fresh sheets have been spread and tucked tight, childhood rooms
    have been seen to,
for this is the season when children return with their children
to the place of Bingham's Ghost, of the Old Timber Wharf, of
    the Big Flood That Time,
the country of the rationalized farms, of the day-and-night farms,
    and of the Pitt Street farms,
of the Shire Engineer and many other rumours, of the tractor
    crankcase furred with chaff,
the places of sitting down near ferns, the snake-fear places, the
    cattle-crossing-long-ago places.

2

It is the season of the Long Narrow City; it has crossed the Myall,
    it has entered the North Coast,
that big stunning snake; it is looped through the hills, burning
    all night there.
Hitching and flying on the downgrades, processionally balancing
    on the climbs,
it echoes in O'Sullivan's Gap, in the tight coats of the flooded-
    gum trees;
the tops of palms exclaim at it unmoved, there near Wootton.
Glowing all night behind the hills, with a north-shifting glare,
    burning behind the hills;
through Coolongolook, through Wang Wauk, across the
    Wallamba,
the booming tarred pipe of the holiday slows and spurts again;
    Nabiac chokes in glassy wind,

the forests on Kiwarric dwindle in cheap light; Tuncurry and
　　Forster swell like cooking oil.
The waiting is buffed, in timber villages off the highway, the
　　waiting is buffeted:
the fumes of fun hanging above ferns; crime flashes in strange
　　windscreens, in the time of the Holiday.
Parasites weave quickly through the long gut that paddocks
　　shine into;
powerful makes surging and pouncing: the police, collecting
　　Revenue.
The heavy gut winds over the Manning, filling northward,
　　digesting the towns, feeding the towns;
they all become the narrow city, they join it;
girls walking close to murder discard, with excitement, their
　　names.
Crossing Australia of the sports, the narrow city, bringing home
　　the children.

3

It is good to come out after driving and walk on bare grass;
walking out, looking all around, relearning that country.
Looking out for snakes, and looking out for rabbits as well;
going into the shade of myrtles to try their cupped climate,
　　swinging by one hand around them,
in that country of the Holiday...
stepping behind trees to the dam, as if you had a gun,
to that place of the Wood Duck,
to that place of the Wood Duck's Nest,
proving you can still do it; looking at the duck who hasn't seen
　　you,
the mother duck who'd run Catch Me (broken wing) I'm Fatter
　　(broken wing), having hissed to her children.

4

The birds saw us wandering along.

Rosellas swept up crying out *we think we think*; they settled farther along;

knapping seeds off the grass, under dead trees where their eggs were, walking around on their fingers,

flying on into the grass.

The heron lifted up his head and elbows; the magpie stepped aside a bit,

angling his chopsticks into pasture, turning things over in his head.

At the place of the Plough Handles, of the Apple Trees Bending Over, and of the Cattlecamp,

there the vealers are feeding; they are loosely at work, facing everywhere.

They are always out there, and the forest is always on the hills;

around the sun are turning the wedgetail eagle and her mate, that dour brushhook-faced family:

they settled on Deer's Hill away back when the sky was opened,

in the bull-oak trees way up there, the place of fur tufted in the grass, the place of bone-turds.

5

The Fathers and the Great-Grandfathers, they are out in the paddocks all the time, they live out there,

at the place of the Rail Fence, of the Furrows Under Grass, at the place of the Slab Chimney.

We tell them that clearing is complete, an outdated attitude, all over;

we preach without a sacrifice, and are ignored; flowering bushes grow dull to our eyes.

We begin to go up on the ridge, talking together, looking at the kino-coloured ants,

at the yard-wide sore of their nest, that kibbled peak, and the workers heaving vast stalks up there,

the brisk compact workers; jointed soldiers pour out then, tense with acid; several probe the mouth of a lost gin bottle:

Innuendo, we exclaim, *literal minds!* and go on up the ridge,
    announced by finches;

passing the place of the Dingo Trap, and that farm hand it caught,
    and the place of the Cowbails,

we come to the road and watch heifers,

little unjoined devons, their teats hidden in fur, and the cousin
    with his loose-slung stockwhip driving them.

We talk with him about rivers and the lakes; his polished horse
    is stepping nervously,

printing neat omegas in the gravel, flexing its skin to shake off
    flies;

his big sidestepping horse that has kept its stones; it recedes
    gradually, bearing him;

we murmur *stone-horse* and *devilry* to the grinners under grass.

6

Barbecue smoke is rising at Legge's Camp; it is steaming into
    the midday air,

all around the lake shore, at the Broadwater, it is going up among
    the paperbark trees,

a heat-shimmer of sauces, rising from tripods and flat steel, at
    that place of the Cone-shells,

at that place of the Seagrass, and the tiny segmented things
    swarming in it, and of the Pelican.

Dogs are running around disjointedly; water escapes from their
    mouths,

confused emotions from their eyes; humans snarl at them
    Gwanout and Hereboy, not varying their tone much;

the impoverished dog people, suddenly sitting down to nuzzle
    themselves; toddlers side with them:

toddlers, running away purposefully at random, among cars,
    into big drownie-water (come back, Cheryl-Ann!).

They rise up as charioteers, leaning back on the tow-bar; all their
    attributes bulge at once;

swapping swash shoulder-wings for the white-sheeted shoes
    that bear them,

they are skidding over the flat glitter, stiff with grace, for once not travelling to arrive.

From the high dunes over there, the rough blue distance, at
length they come back behind the boats,

and behind the boats' noise, cartwheeling, or sitting down,
into the lake's warm chair;

they wade ashore and eat with the families, putting off that
up-rightness, that assertion,

eating with the families who love equipment, and the freedom
from equipment,

with the fathers who love driving, and lighting a fire between
stones.

7

Shapes of children were moving in the standing corn, in the
child-labour districts;

coloured flashes of children, between the green and parching
stalks, appearing and disappearing.

Some places, they are working, racking off each cob like a lever,
tossing it on the heaps;

other places, they are children of child-age, there playing
jungle:

in the tiger-striped shade, they are firing hoehandle machine
guns, taking cover behind fat pumpkins;

in other cases, it is Sunday and they are lovers.

They rise and walk together in the sibilance, finding single rows
irksome, hating speech now,

or, full of speech, they swap files and follow defiles, disappearing
and appearing;

near the rain-grey barns, and the children building cattleyards
beside them;

the standing corn, gnawed by pouched and rodent mice;
generations are moving among it.

the parrot-hacked, medicine-tasseled corn, ascending all the
creek flats, the wire-fenced alluvials.

going up in patches through the hills, towards the Steep Country.

8

Forests and State Forests, all down off the steeper country;
mosquitoes are always living in there:
they float about like dust motes and sink down, at the places
of the Stinging Tree,
and of the Staghorn Fern; the males feed on plant-stem fluid,
absorbing that watery ichor;
the females meter the air, feeling for the warm-blooded smell,
needing blood for their eggs.
They find the dingo in his sleeping-place, they find his under-
belly and his anus;
they find the possum's face, they drift up the ponderous pleats
of the fig tree, way up into its rigging,
the high camp of the fruit bats; they feed on the membranes and
ears of bats; tired wings cuff air at them;
their eggs burning inside them, they alight on the muzzles of
cattle,
the half-wild bush cattle, there at the place of the Sleeper Dump,
at the place of the Tallowwoods.
The males move about among growth tips; ingesting solutions,
they crouch intently;
the females sing, needing blood to breed their young; their singing
is in the scrub country;
their tune comes to the name-bearing humans, who dance to it
and irritably grin at it.

9

The warriors are cutting timber with brash chainsaws; they are
trimming hardwood pit-props and loading them;
Is that an order? they hoot at the peremptory lorry driver, who
laughs; he is also a warrior.
They are driving long-nosed tractors, slashing pasture in the
dinnertime sun;
they are fitting tappets and valves, the warriors, or giving finish
to a surfboard.
Addressed on the beach by a pale man, they watch waves break
and are reserved, refusing pleasantry;

they joke only with fellow warriors, chaffing about try-ons and
the police, not slighting women.
Making Timber a word of power, Con-rod a word of power,
Sense a word of power, the Regs. a word of power,
they know belt-fed from spring-fed; they speak of being *stiff*,
and being *history*;
the warriors who have killed, and the warriors who eschewed
killing,
the solemn, the drily spoken, the life peerage of endurance;
drinking water from a tap,
they watch boys who think hard work a test, and boys who think
it is not a test.

10

Now the ibis are flying in, hovering down on the wetlands,
on those swampy paddocks around Darawank, curving down
in ragged dozens,
on the riverside flats along the Wang Wauk, on the Boolambayte
pasture flats,
and away towards the sea, on the sand moors, at the place of the
Jabiru Crane.
Leaning out of their wings, they step down; they take out their
implement at once,
out of its straw wrapping, and start work; they dab grasshopper
and ground-cricket
with nonexistence...spiking the ground and puncturing it...they
swallow down the outcry of a frog;
they discover titbits kept for them under cowmanure lids, small
slow things.
Pronging the earth, they make little socket noises, their thought-
fulness jolting down-and-up suddenly;
there at Bunyah, along Firefly Creek, and up through Germany,
the ibis are all at work again, thin-necked ageing men towards
evening; they are solemnly all back
at Minimbah, and on the Manning, in the rye-and-clover irrigation
fields;
city storemen and accounts clerks point them out to their wives,
remembering things about themselves, and about the ibis.

11

Abandoned fruit trees, moss-tufted, spotted with dim lichen
     paints; the fruit trees of the Grandmothers,
they stand along the creekbanks, in the old home paddocks,
     where the houses were;
they are reached through bramble-grown front gates, they creak
     at dawn behind burnt skillions,
at Belbora, at Bucca Wauka, away in at Burrell Creek,
at Telararee of the gold-sluices.
The trees are split and rotten-elbowed; they bear the old-fashioned
     summer fruits,
the annual bygones: china pear, quince, persimmon;
the fruit has the taste of former lives, of sawdust and parlour
     song, the tang of Manners;
children bite it, recklessly,
at what will become for them the place of the Slab Wall, and of
     the Coal Oil Lamp,
the place of moss-grit and swallows' nests, the place of the
     Crockery.

12

Now the sun is an applegreen blindness through the swells, a
     white blast on the sea-face, flaking and shoaling;
now it is burning off the mist; it is emptying the density of trees,
     it is spreading upriver,
hovering above the casuarina needles, there at Old Bar and
     Manning Point;
flooding the island farms, it abolishes the milkers' munching
     breath
as they walk towards the cowyards; it stings a bucket here, a
     teatcup there.
Morning steps into the world by ever more southerly gates;
     shadows weaken their north skew
on Middle Brother, on Cape Hawke, on the dune scrub toward
     Seal Rocks;
steadily the heat is coming on, the butter-water time, the clothes-
     sticking time;

grass covers itself with straw; abandoned things are thronged
with spirits;

everywhere wood is still with strain; birds hiding down the creek
galleries, and in the cockspur canes;

the cicada is hanging up her sheets; she takes wing off her music-
sheets.

Cars pass with a rational zoom, panning quickly towards
Wingham,

through the thronged and glittering, the shale-topped ridges,
and the cattlecamps,

towards Wingham for the cricket, the ball knocked hard in front
of smoked-glass ranges, and for the drinking.

In the time of heat, the time of flies around the mouth, the time
of the west verandah;

looking at that umbrage along the ranges, on the New England
side;

clouds begin assembling vaguely, a hot soiled heaviness on the
sky, away there towards Gloucester;

a swelling up of clouds, growing there above Mount George,
and above Tipperary;

far away and hot with light; sometimes a storm takes root there,
and fills the heavens rapidly;

darkening, boiling up and swaying on its stalks, pulling this way
and that, blowing round by Krambach;

coming white on Bulby, it drenches down on the paddocks, and
on the wire fences;

the paddocks are full of ghosts, and people in cornbag hoods
approaching;

lights are lit in the house; the storm veers mightily on its stem,
above the roof; the hills uphold it;

the stony hills guide its dissolution; gullies opening and crumbling
down, wrenching tussocks and rolling them;

the storm carries a greenish-grey bag; perhaps it will find hail and
send it down, starring cars, flattening tomatoes,

in the time of the Washaways, of the dead trunks braiding water,
and of the Hailstone Yarns.

13

The stars of the holiday step out all over the sky.

People look up at them, out of their caravan doors and their
     campsites;

people look up from the farms, before going back; they gaze at
     their year's worth of stars.

The Cross hangs head-downward, out there over Markwell;

it turns upon the Still Place, the pivot of the Seasons, with one
     shoulder rising:

"Now I'm beginning to rise, with my Pointers and my Load..."

hanging eastwards, it shines on the sawmills and the lakes, on
     the glasses of the Old People.

Looking at the Cross, the galaxy is over our left shoulder, slung
     up highest in the east;

there the Dog is following the Hunter; the Dog Star pulsing there
     above Forster; it shines down on the Bikies,

and on the boat-hire sheds, there at the place of the Oyster; the
     place of the Shark's Eggs and her Hide;

the Pleiades are pinned up high on the darkness, away back
     above the Manning;

they are shining on the Two Blackbutt Trees, on the rotted river
     wharves, and on the towns;

standing there, above the water and the lucerne flats, at the place
     of the Families;

their light sprinkles down on Taree of the Lebanese shops, it
     mingles with the streetlights and their glare.

People recover the starlight, hitching north,

travelling north beyond the seasons, into that country of the
     Communes, and of the Banana:

the Flying Horse, the Rescued Girl, and the Bull, burning steadily
     above that country.

Now the New Moon is low down in the west, that remote direction
     of the Cattlemen,

and of the Saleyards, the place of steep clouds, and of the Rodeo;

the New Moon who has poured out her rain, the moon of the
     Planting-times.

People go outside and look at the stars, and at the melon-rind
     moon,

the Scorpion going down into the mountains, over there towards
    Waukivory, sinking into the tree-line,
in the time of the Rockmelons, and of the Holiday...
the Cross is rising on his elbow, above the glow of the horizon;
carrying a small star in his pocket, he reclines there brilliantly,
above the Alum Mountain, and the lakes threaded on the Myall
    River, and above the Holiday.

The Gum Forest

After the last gapped wire on a post,
homecoming for me, to enter the gum forest.

This old slow battlefield: parings of armour,
cracked collars, elbows, scattered on the ground.

New trees step out of old: lemon and ochre
splitting out of grey everywhere, in the gum forest.

In there for miles, shade track and ironbark slope,
depth casually beginning all around, at a little distance.

Sky sifting, and always a hint of smoke in the light;
you can never reach the heart of the gum forest.

In here is like a great yacht harbour, charmed to leaves,
innumerable tackle, poles wrapped in spattered sail,
or an unknown army in reserve for centuries.

Flooded-gums on creek ground, each tall because of each.
Now a blackbutt in bloom is showering with bees
but warm blood sleeps in the middle of the day.
The witching hour is noon in the gum forest.

Foliage builds like a layering splash: ground water
drily upheld in edge-on, wax-rolled, gall-puckered
leaves upon leaves. The shoal life of parrots up there.

63

Stone footings, trunk-shattered. Non-human lights. Enormous
abandoned machines. The mysteries of the gum forest.

Delight to me, though, at the water-smuggling creeks,
health to me, too, under banksia candles and combs.

A wind is up, rubbing limbs above the bullock roads;
mountains are waves in the ocean of the gum forest.

I go my way, looking back sometimes, looking round me;
singed oils clear my mind, and the pouring sound high up.

Why have I denied the passions of my time? To see
lightning strike upward out of the gum forest.

The Future

There is nothing about it. Much science fiction is set there
but is not about it. Prophecy is not about it.
It sways no yarrow stalks. And crystal is a mirror.
Even the man we nailed on a tree for a lookout
said little about it; he told us evil would come.
We see, by convention, a small living distance into it
but even that's a projection. And all our projections
fail to curve where it curves.
                               It is the black hole
out of which no radiation escapes to us.
The commonplace and magnificent roads of our lives
go on some way through cityscape and landscape
or steeply sloping, or scree, into that sheer fall
where everything will be that we have ever sent there,
compacted, spinning – except perhaps us, to see it.
It is said we see the start.
                               But, from here, there's a blindness.
The side-heaped chasm that will swallow all our present
blinds us to the normal sun that may be imagined

shining calmly away on the far side of it, for others
in their ordinary day. A day to which all our portraits,
ideals, revolutions, denim and deshabille
are quaintly heartrending. To see those people is impossible,
to greet them, mawkish. Nonetheless, I begin:
"When I was alive –"
                         and I am turned around
to find myself looking at a cheerful picnic party,
the women decently legless, in muslin and gloves,
the men in beards and weskits, with the long
cheroots and duck trousers of the better sort,
relaxing on a stone verandah. Ceylon, or Sydney.
And as I look, I know they are utterly gone,
each one on his day, with pillow, small bottles, mist,
with all the futures they dreamed or dealt in, going
down to that engulfment everything approaches;
with the man on the tree, they have vanished into the Future.

Immigrant Voyage

My wife came out on the *Goya*
in the mid-year of our century.

In the fogs of that winter
many hundred ships were sounding;
the DP camps were being washed to sea.

The bombsites and the ghettoes
were edging out to Israel,
to Brazil, to Africa, America.

The separating ships were bound away
to the cities of refuge
built for the age of progress.

Hull-down and pouring light
the tithe-barns, the cathedrals
were bearing the old castes away.

O

Pattern-bombed out of babyhood,
Hungarians-become-Swiss,
the children heard their parents:
Argentina? Or Australia?
Less politics, in Australia...

Dark Germany, iron frost
and the waiting many weeks
then a small converted warship
under the moon, turning south.

Way beyond the first star
and beyond Cap Finisterre
the fishes and the birds
did eat of their heave-offerings.

O

The *Goya* was a barracks:
mess-queue, spotlights, tower,
crossing the Middle Sea.

In the haunted blue light
that burned nightlong in the sleeping-decks
the tiered bunks were restless
with coughing, demons, territory.

On the Sea of Sweat, the Red Sea,
the flat heat melted even
dulled deference of the injured.
Nordics and Slavonics
paid salt-tax day and night, being
absolved of Europe

66

but by the Gate of Tears
the barrack was a village
with accordeons and dancing
(Fräulein, kennen Sie meinen Rhythmus?)
approaching the southern stars.

O

Those who said Europe
has fallen to the Proles
and the many who said
we are going for the children,

the nouveau poor
and the cheerful shirtsleeve Proles,

the children, who thought
No Smoking signs meant men
mustn't dress for dinner,

those who had hopes
and those who knew that they
were giving up their lives

were becoming the people
who would say, and sometimes urge,
in the English-speaking years;
we came out on the *Goya*.

O

At last, a low coastline,
old horror of Dutch sail-captains.

Behind it, still unknown,
sunburnt farms, strange trees, family jokes
and all the classes of equality.

As it fell away northwards
there was one last week for songs,
for dreaming at the rail,
for beloved meaningless words.

Standing in to Port Phillip
in the salt-grey summer light
the village dissolved
into strained shapes holding luggage;

now they, like the dour
Australians below them, were facing
encounter with the Foreign
where all subtlety fails.

O

Those who, with effort,
with concealment, with silence, had resisted
the collapsed star Death,
who had clawed their families from it,
those crippled by that gravity

were suddenly, shockingly
being loaded aboard lorries:
They say, another camp –
One did not come for this –

As all the refitted
ships stood, oiling, in the Bay,
spectres, furious and feeble,
accompanied the trucks through Melbourne,

resignation, understandings
that cheerful speed dispelled at length.

That first day, rolling north
across the bright savanna,
not yet people, but numbers.
Population. Forebears.

O

Bonegilla, Nelson Bay,
the dry-land barbed wire ships
from which some would never land.

In these, as their parents
learned the Fresh Start music:
physicians nailing crates
attorneys cleaning trams,
the children had one last
ambiguous summer holiday.

Ahead of them lay
the Deep End of the schoolyard,
tribal testing, tribal soft-drinks,
and learning English fast,
the Wang-Wang language.

Ahead of them, refinements:
thumbs hooked down hard under belts
to repress gesticulation;

ahead of them, epithets:
wog, reffo, Commo Nazi,
things which can be forgotten
but must first be told.

And farther ahead
in the years of the Coffee Revolution
and the Smallgoods Renaissance,
the early funerals:

the misemployed, the unadaptable;
those marked by the Abyss,

friends who came on the *Goya*
in the mid-year of our century.

The Grassfire Stanzas

August, and black centres expand on the afternoon paddock.
Dilating on a match in widening margins, they lift
a splintering murmur; they fume out of used-up grass
that's been walked, since summer, into infinite swirled licks.

The man imposing spring here swats with his branch, controlling
     it:
only small things may come to a head, in this settlement pattern.

Fretted with small flame, the aspiring islands leave
odd plumes behind. Smuts shower up every thermal
to float down long stairs. Aggregate smoke attracts a kestrel.

Eruption of darkness from far down under roots
is the aspect of these cores, on the undulating farmland;
dense black is withered into web, inside a low singing;
it is dried and loosened, on the surface; it is made weak.

The green feed that shelters beneath its taller death yearly
is unharmed, under now loaf soot. Arriving hawks teeter
and plunge continually, working over the hopping outskirts.

The blackenings are balanced, on a gradient of dryness
in the almost-still air, between dying thinly away
and stripping the whole countryside. Joining, they never gain
more than they lose. They spread away from their high moments.

The man carries smoke wrapped in bark, and keeps applying it
starting new circles. He is burning the passive ocean
around his ark of buildings and his lifeboat water;

it wasn't this man, but it was man, sing the agile
exclamatory birds, who taught them this rapt hunting
(strike! in the updrafts, snap! of hardwood pods).
Humans found the fire here. It is inherent. They learn,
wave after wave of them, how to touch the country.

Sterilizing reed distaffs, the fire edges on to a dam;
it circuits across a cow-track; new surf starts riding outward
and a nippy kestrel feeds from its foot, over cooling mergers.

It's the sun that is touched, and dies in expansion, mincing,
making the round dance, foretelling its future, driving
the frantic lives outwards. The sun that answers the bark tip
is discharged in many little songs, to forestall a symphony.

Cattle come, with stilted bounding calves. They look across the
ripple lines of heat, and shake their armed heads at them;
at random, then, they step over. Grazing smudged black country
they become the beasts of Tartarus. Wavering, moving out over
dung-smouldering ground still covered with its uncovering.

Homage to the Launching Place

Pleasure-craft of the sprung rhythms, bed,
                    kindest of quadrupeds,
you are also the unrocking boat
                    that moves on silence.

Straining hatchway into this world,
                    you sustain our collapses
above earth; guarantor of evolution,
                    you are our raised base-line.

Resisting gravity, for us and in us,
                    you form a planet-wide
unobtrusive discontinuous platform,
                    a layer: the mattressphere,

pretty nearly our highest common level
                    (tables may dispute it).

Muscles' sweatprinted solace,
godmother of butt-stubbing dreams,
                    you sublimate, Great Vehicle,
all our upright passions;

                    midwife of figuring, and design,
you moderate them wisely;
                    aiming solitude outwards, at action,
you sigh Think some more. Sleep on it...

Solitude. Approaching rest
Time reveals her oscillation
                    and narrows into space;
                    there is time in that dilation:
                    Mansions. Defiles. Continents.
                    The living and the greatly living,

                    objects that take sides,
                    that aren't morally neutral

you accept my warm absence
                    there, as you will accept,
one day, my cooling presence.

                    I loved you from the first, bed,
doorway out of this world;
                    above your inner springs
I learned to dig my own.
                    Primly dressed, linen-collared one,
you look so still, for your speed,
                    shield that carries us to the fight
                    and bears us from it.

First Essay on Interest

Not usury, but interest. The cup slowed in mid-raise,
the short whistle, hum, the little forwards shift
mark our intake of that non-physical breath

which the lungs mimic sharply, to cancel the gap in pressure
left by our self vanishing into its own alert –
A blink returns us to self, that intimate demeanour

self-repairing as a bow-wave. What we have received
is the ordinary mail of the otherworld, wholly common,
not postmarked divine; no one refuses delivery,

not even the eagle, her face fixed at heavy Menace:
I have juices to sort the relevant from the irrelevant;
even her gaze may tilt left, askance, aloof, right,
fixing a still unknown. Delaying huge flight.

Interest. Mild and inherent with fire as oxygen,
it is a sporadic inhalation. We can live long days
under its surface, breathing material air

then something catches, is itself. Intent and special silence.
This is interest, that blinks our interests out
and alone permits their survival, by relieving

us of their gravity, for a timeless moment;
that centres where it points, and points to centering,
that centres us where it points, and reflects our centre.

It is a form of love. The everyday shines through it
and patches of time. But it does not mingle with these;
it wakens only for each trace in them of the Beloved.

And this breath of interest is non-rhythmical:
it is human to obey, humane to be wary of rhythm
as tainted by the rallies, as marching with the snare drum.
The season of interest is not fixed in the calendar cycle;

it pulls towards acute dimensions. Death is its intimate.
When that Holland of cycles, the body, veers steeply downhill
interest retreats from the face; it ceases to instill
and fade, like breath; it becomes a vivid steady state

that registers every grass-blade seen on the way,
the long combed grain in the steps, free insects flying;
it stands aside from your panic, the wracked disarray;
it behaves as if it were the part of you not dying.

Affinity of interest with extremity
seems to distil to this polar disaffinity
that suggests the beloved is not death, but rather
what our death has hidden. Which may be this world.

The Fishermen at South Head

They have walked out as far as they can go on the prow of the
    continent,
on the undercut white sandstone, the bowsprits of the towering
    headland.

They project their long light canes
or raise them up to check and string, like quiet archers.
Between casts they hold them couched,
a finger on the line, two fingers on a cigarette, the reel cocked.

They watch the junction of smooth blue with far matt-shining
    blue,
the join where clouds enter,
or they watch the wind-shape of their nylon
bend like a sail's outline
south towards, a mile away, the city's floating gruel
of gull-blown effluent.

Sometimes they glance north, at the people on that calf-coloured
    edge
lower than theirs, where the suicides come by taxi
and stretchers are winched up
later, under raining lights
but mostly their eyes stay level with the land-and-ocean glitter.

74

Where they stand, atop the centuries
of strata, they don't look down much
but feel through their tackle the talus-eddying
and tidal detail of that huge simple pulse
in the rock and in their bones.

Through their horizontal poles they divine the creatures of ocean:
a touch, a dip, and a busy winding death gets started;
hands will turn for minutes, rapidly,
before, still opening its pitiful doors, the victim
dawns above the rim, and is hoisted in a flash above the suburbs
– or before the rod flips, to stand
trailing sworn-at gossamer.

On that highest dreadnought scarp, where the terra cotta
waves of bungalows stop, suspended at sky,
the hunters stand apart.
They encourage one another, at a distance, not by talk

but by being there, by unhooking now and then
a twist of silver for the creel, by a vaguely mutual
zodiac of cars TV windcheaters.
Braced, casual normality. Anything unshared,
a harlequin mask, a painted wand flourished at the sun
would anger them. It is serious to be with humans.

The Sydney Highrise Variations

1. FUEL STOPPAGE ON GLADESVILLE ROAD BRIDGE IN THE YEAR 1980

So we're sitting over our sick beloved engine
atop a great building of the double century
on the summit that exhilarates cars, the concrete vault on
                                        its thousands
of tonnes of height, far above the tidal turnaround.

Gigantic pure form, all exterior, superbly uninhabited
or peopled only by transients at speed, the bridge
is massive outline.

                It was inked in by scaffolding and workers.
Seen from itself, the arch
is an abstract hill, a roadway up-and-over without country,
from below, a ponderous grotto, all entrance and vast shade
framing blues and levels.

From a distance, the flyover on its vaulting drum
is a sketched stupendous ground-burst, a bubble raising surface
or a rising heatless sun with inset horizons.

                    Also it's a space-probe,
a trajectory of strange fixed dusts, that were milled,
boxed with steel rod mesh and fired, in stages,
from sandstone point to point. They docked at apogee.

It feels good. It feels right.
The joy of sitting high is in our judgement.
The marvellous brute-force effects of our century work.
They answer something in us. Anything in us.

2   VIEW OF SYDNEY, AUSTRALIA, FROM GLADESVILLE ROAD BRIDGE

There's that other great arch eastward, with its hanging high-
     ways;
the headlands and horizons of packed suburb, white among
     bisque-fired; odd smokes rising;
there's Warrang, the flooded valley, that is now the ship-chained
     Harbour,
recurrent everywhere, with its azure and its grains;
ramped parks, bricked containers,
verandahs successive around walls,
and there's the central highrise, multi-storey, the twenty-year
     countdown,
the new city standing on its haze above the city.

Ingots of shear
affluence poles
bomb-drawing grid
of columnar profit
piecrust and scintillant
tunnels in the sky
high window printouts
repeat their lines
repeat their lines
repeat their lines
credit conductors
bar graphs on blue
glass tubes of boom
in concrete wicker
each trade Polaris
government Agena
fine print insurrected
tall drinks on a tray

All around them is the old order: brewery brick terrace hospital
horrible workplace; the scale of the tramway era,
the peajacket era, the age of the cliff-repeating woolstores.
South and west lie the treeless suburbs, a mulch of faded flags,
north and partly east, the built-in paradise forest.

3   THE FLIGHT FROM MANHATTAN

It is possible the heights of this view are a museum:
though the highrise continues desultorily along some ridges,
        canned Housing, Strata Title,
        see-through Office Space,
        upright bedsteads of Harbour View,
        residential soviets,
the cranes have all but vanished from the central upsurge.

        Hot-air money-driers,
        towering double entry,
        Freud's cobwebbed poem
        with revolving restaurant,

they took eighty years to fly here from Manhattan
these variant towers. By then, they were arriving everywhere.

      In the land of veneers,
      of cladding, of Cape Codding
      (I shall have Cope Codded)
      they put on heavy side.

The iron ball was loose in the old five-storey city
clearing bombsites for them. They rose like nouveaux accents
and stilled for a time, the city's conversation.

      Their arrival paralleled
      the rise of the Consumers
      gazing through themselves
      at iconoclasms, wines,
      Danish Modern ethics.

Little we could love expanded to fill the spaces
of high glazed prosperity. An extensive city
that had long contained the dimensions of heaven and hell
couldn't manage total awe at the buildings of the Joneses.

      Their reign coincided
      with an updraft of Ideology,
      that mood in which the starving
      spirit is fed upon the heart.

Employment and neckties and ruling themes ascended
into the towers. But they never filled them.
Squinting at them through the salt
and much-washed glass of her history, the city kept her flavour
fire-ladder high, rarely above three storeys.

In ambiguous battle at length, she began to hedge
the grilles of Aspiration. To limit them to standing
on economic grounds. With their twists of sculpture.

On similar grounds we are stopped here, still surveying
the ridgy plain of houses. Enormous. England's buried Gulag.
The stacked entrepôt, great city of the Australians.

4   THE C19-20

The Nineteenth Century. The Twentieth Century.
There were never any others. No centuries before these.
Dante was not hailed in his time as an Authentic
Fourteenth Century Voice. Nor did Cromwell thunder After all,
in the bowels of Christ, this *is* the Seventeenth Century.

The two are one aircraft in the end, the C19-20,
capacious with cargo. Some of it can save your life,
some can prevent it.
The cantilevered behemoth
is fitted up with hospitals and electric Gatling guns
to deal with recalcitrant and archaic spirits.

It rose out of the Nineteenth, steam pouring from venturi
and every man turning hay with a wooden fork
in the Age of Piety (A.D. or B.C.) wants one
in his nation's airline. And his children dream of living
in a palace of packing crates beside the cargo terminal:
No one will see! Everything will be surprises!

Directly under the flightpath, and tuned to listening,
we hear the cockpit traffic, the black box channel
that can't be switched off: Darwinians and Lawrentians
are wrestling for the controls,
We must take her into Space! / We must fly in potent circles!

5   THE RECESSION OF THE JONESES

The worldwide breath of Catching Up
may serve to keep the mighty, slowing
machine aloft beyond our lifetime:
nearly all of the poor are blowing.

The soaring double century
might end, and mutate, and persist;
as we've been speaking, the shadows of
bridges, cranes, towers have shifted east.

When we create our own high style
skill and the shadow will not then part;
as rhetoric would conceal from art
effort has at best a winning margin.

The sun, that is always catching up
with night and day and month and year
blazes from its scrolled bare face *To be
solar, I must be nuclear –*

Six hundred glittering and genteel towns
gathered to be urban in plein air,
more complex in their levels than their heights
and vibrant with modernity's strange anger.

Quintets for Robert Morley

Is it possible that hyper-
ventilating up Parnassus
I have neglected to pay tribute
to the Stone Age aristocracy?
    I refer to the fat.

We were probably the earliest
civilized, and civilizing, humans,
the first to win the leisure,
sweet boredom, life-enhancing sprawl
    that require style.

Tribesfolk spared us and cared for us
for good reasons. Our reasons.
As age's counterfeits, forerunners of the city
we survived, and multiplied. Out of self-defence
   we invented the Self.

It's likely we also invented some of love,
much of fertility (see the Willensdorf Venus)
parts of theology (divine feasting, Unmoved Movers)
likewise complexity, stateliness, the ox-cart
   and self-deprecation.

Not that the lists of pugnacity are bare
of stout fellows. Ask a Sumo.
Warriors taunt us still, and fear us:
in heroic war, we are apt to be the specialists
   and the generals.

But we do better in peacetime. For ourselves
we would spare the earth. We were the first moderns
after all, being like the Common Man
disqualified from tragedy. Accessible to shame, though,
   subtler than the tall,

we make reasonable rulers.
Never trust a lean meritocracy
nor the leader who has been lean;
only the lifelong big have the knack of wedding
   greatness with balance.

Never wholly trust the fat man
who lurks in the lean achiever
and in the defeated, yearning to get out.
He has not been through our initiations,
   he lacks the light feet.

Our having life abundantly
is equivocal, Robert, in hot climates
where the hungry watch us. I lack the light step then.
How many of us, I wonder, walk those streets
    in terrible disguise?

So much climbing, on a spherical world;
had Newton not been a mere beginner at gravity
he might have asked how the apple got up there
in the first place. And so might have discerned
    an ampler physics.

The New Moreton Bay
(on the conversion to Catholicism of the poet Kevin Hart)

A grog-primed overseer, who later died,
snapped at twenty convicts gasping in a line
That pole ain't heavy! Two men stand aside!
and then two more, *and you, pop-eyes! And you!*
– until the dozen left, with a terrible cry,
broke and were broken
beneath the tons of log they had stemmed aloft desperately.

Because there is no peace in this world's peace
the timber is to carry. Many hands heave customarily,
some step aside, detained by the Happiness Police
or despair's boutiques; it is a continual sway –
but when grace and intent
recruit a fresh shoulder, then we're in the other testament
and the innocent wood lifts line-long, with its leaves and libraries.

Bent Water in the Tasmanian Highlands

Flashy wrists out of buttoned grass cuffs, feral whisky burning
  gravels,
jazzy knuckles ajitter on soakages, peaty cupfulls, soft pots
  overflowing,
setting out along the great curve, migrating mouse-quivering
  water,
mountain-driven winter water, in the high tweed, stripping off
  its mountains
to run faster in its skin, it swallows the above, it feeds where it
  is fed on,
it forms at many points and creases outwards, pleated water
shaking out its bedding soil, increasing its scale, beginning the
  headlong
– Bent Water, you could call this level
between droplet and planetary, not as steered by twisting beds
  laterally
but as upped and swayed on its swelling and outstanding own
  curvatures,
its floating top that sweeps impacts sidelong, its event-horizon,
a harelip round a pebble, mouthless cheeks globed over a boulder, a
finger's far-stretched holograph, skinned flow athwart a snag
– these flexures are all reflections, motion-glyphs, pitches of
  impediment,
say a log commemorated in a log-long hump of wave,
a buried rock continually noted, a squeeze-play
through a cracked basalt bar, maintaining a foam-roofed two-
  sided
overhang of breakneck riesling; uplifted hoseless hosings, fully
  circular water,
flattened water off rock sills, sandwiched between an upper
and a lower whizzing surface, trapped in there with airy scatter
and mingled high-speed mirrorings; water groined, produced
  and spiralled
– Crowded scrollwork from events, at steepening white velocities
as if the whole outline of the high country were being pulled
  out

along these joining channels, and proving infinite, anchored
    deeply as it is
in the groundwater scale, in the silence around racy breccia
yet it is spooling out; the great curve, drawing and driving,
of which these are the animal-sized swells and embodiments
won't always describe this upland; and after the jut falls, the
    inverse
towering on gorges, these peaks will be hidden beneath
rivers and tree-bark, in electricity, in cattle, on the ocean
– Meditation is a standing wave, though, on the black-green
    inclines
of pouring and cascading, slate-dark rush and timber-worker's
    tea
bullying the pebble-fans; if we were sketched first at this speed,
sheaths, buttocks, wings, it is mother and history and swank
    here
till our wave is drained of water. And as such it includes the
    writhing
down in a trench, knees, bellies, the struggling, the slack bleeding
remote enough perhaps, within its close clean film
to make the observer a god; do we come here to be gods?
or to watch an alien pouring down the slants of our anomaly
and be hypnotized to rest by it? So much detail's unlikely, for
    hypnosis;
it looks like brotherhood sought at a dreamer's remove
and, in either view, laws of falling and persistence:
the continuous ocean round a planetary stone, braiding uptilts
after swoops, echo-forms, arches built from above and standing
on flourish, clear storeys, translucent honey-glazed clerestories –

Equanimity

Nests of golden porridge shattered in the silky-oak trees,
cobs and crusts of it, their glory-box;
the jacarandas' open violet immensities
mirrored flat on the lawns,
weighted by sprinklers; birds, singly and in flocks

hopping over the suburb, eating, as birds do, in detail
and paying their peppercorns;
talk of "the good life" tangles love with will
however; if we mention it, there is more to say:
the droughty light, for example, at telephone-wire
height above the carports, not the middle-ground
distilling news-photograph light of a smoggy Wednesday,
but that light of the north-west wind, hung on the sky
like the haze above cattleyards;
hungry mountain birds, too, drifting in for food, with the sound
of moist gullies about them, and the sound of the pinch-bar;
we must hear the profoundly unwished
garble of a neighbours' quarrel, and see repeatedly
the face we saw near the sportswear shop today
in which mouth-watering and tears couldn't be distinguished.

Fire-prone place-names apart
there is only love; there are no Arcadias.
Whatever its variants of meat-cuisine, worship, divorce,
human order has at heart
an equanimity. Quite different from inertia, it's a place
where the churchman's not defensive, the indignant aren't
                        on the qui vive,
the loser has lost interest, the accountant is truant to remorse,
where the farmer has done enough struggling-to-survive
for one day, and the artist rests from theory –
where all are, in short, off the high comparative horse
of their identity.
Almost beneath notice, as attainable as gravity, it is
a continuous recovering moment. Pity the high madness
that misses it continually, ranging without rest between
assertion and unconsciousness,
the sort that makes hell seem a height of evolution.
Through the peace beneath effort
(even within effort: quiet air between the bars of our attention)
comes unpurchased lifelong plenishment;
Christ spoke to people most often on this level
especially when they chattered about kingship and the Romans;
all holiness speaks from it.

From the otherworld of action and media, this
interleaved continuing plane is hard to focus:
we are looking into the light –
it makes some smile, some grimace.
More natural to look at the birds about the street, their life
that is greedy, pinched, courageous and prudential
as any on these bricked tree-mingled miles of settlement,
to watch the unceasing on-off
grace that attends their nearly every movement,
the crimson parrot has it, alighting, tips, and recovers it,
the same grace moveless in the shapes of trees
and complex in our selves and fellow walkers: we see it's indivisible
and scarcely willed. That it lights us from the incommensurable
that we sometimes glimpse, from being trapped in the point
(bird minds and ours are so pointedly visual):
a field all foreground, and equally all background,
like a painting of equality. Of definite detailed extent
like God's attention. Where nothing is diminished by perspective.

The Forest Hit by Modern Use

The forest, hit by modern use,
stands graced with damage.
                    Angled plaques
tilt everywhere, with graphic needle crowns
and trinket saps fixed round their year;
vines spiderweb, flowering, over smashed
intricacies; long rides appear.

Dense growths that were always underbrush
expand in the light, beside bulldozers'
imprinted machine-gun belts of spoor.

Now the sun's in, through breaks and jags,
culled slopes are jammed with replacement: green
and whipstick saplings, every one out

to shade the rest to death.
                              Scabbed chain
feeds leaf-mould its taut rain-cold solution;
bared creeks wash gold; kingfishers hover.

There is still great height: all through the hills
spared hierarchs toughen to the wind
around the punk hearts that got them spared
and scatter seed down the logging roads.

Grease-fungi, scrolls, clenched pipes of bark:
the forest will now be kept like this
for a long time. There are rooms in it
and, paradox for mystery, birds
too tiny, now that we see them, for
their amplitude and carrying flash of song.

On a plinth, the sea-eagle eats by lengths
their enemy, a coil-whipping dry land fish
and voids white size to make room for it.

Shower

From the metal poppy
this good blast of trance
arriving as shock, private cloudburst blazing down,
worst in a boarding-house greased tub, or a barrack with
        competitions,
best in a stall, this enveloping passion of Australians:
tropics that sweat for you, torrent that braces with its heat,
inflames you with its chill, action sauna, inverse bidet,
sleek vertical coruscating ghost of your inner river,
reminding all your fluids, streaming off your points, awakening
the tacky soap to blossom and ripe autumn, releasing the squeezed
        gardens,
smoky valet smoothing your impalpable overnight pyjamas off,

pillar you can step through, force-field absolving love's efforts,
nicest yard of the jogging track, speeding aeroplane minutely
steered with two controls, or trimmed with a knurled wheel.
Some people like to still this energy and lie in it,
stirring circles with their pleasure in it – but my delight's that
        toga
worn on either or both shoulders, fluted drapery, silk whispering
        to the tiles
with its spiralling frothy hem continuous round the gurgle-hole;
this ecstatic partner, dreamy to dance in slow embrace with
after factory-floor rock, or even to meet as Lot's abstracted
merciful wife on a rusty ship in dog latitudes,
sweetest dressing of the day in the dusty bush, this persistent
time-capsule of unwinding, this nimble straight well-wisher.
Only in England is its name an unkind word;
only in Europe is it enjoyed by telephone.

The Quality of Sprawl

Sprawl is the quality
of the man who cut down his Rolls Royce
into a farm utility truck, and sprawl
is what the company lacked when it made repeated efforts
to buy the vehicle back and repair its image.

Sprawl is doing your farming by aeroplane, roughly,
or driving a hitchhiker that extra hundred miles home.
It is the rococo of being your own still centre.
It is never lighting cigars with ten-dollar notes:
that's idiot ostentation and murder of starving people.
Nor can it be bought with the ash of million-dollar deeds.

Sprawl lengthens the legs; it trains greyhounds on liver and beer.
Sprawl almost never says Why not? with palms comically raised
nor can it be dressed for, not even in running shoes worn

with mink and a nose ring. That is Society. That's Style.
Sprawl is more like the thirteenth banana in a dozen
or anyway the fourteenth.

Sprawl is Hank Stamper in Never Give an Inch
bisecting an obstructive official's desk with a chain saw.
Not harming the official. Sprawl is never brutal
though it's often intransigent. Sprawl is never Simon de Montfort
at a town-storming: Kill them all! God will know his own.
Knowing the man's name this was said to might be sprawl.

Sprawl occurs in art. The fifteenth to twenty-first
lines in a sonnet, for example. And in certain paintings;
I have sprawl enough to have forgotten which paintings.
Turner's glorious Burning of the Houses of Parliament
comes to mind, a doubling bannered triumph of sprawl –
except, he didn't fire them.

Sprawl gets up the nose of many kinds of people
(every kind that comes in kinds) whose futures don't include it.
Some decry it as criminal presumption, silken-robed Pope
      Alexander
dividing the new world between Spain and Portugal.
If he smiled in petto afterwards, perhaps the thing did have sprawl.

Sprawl is really classless, though. It's John Christopher Frederick
      Murray
asleep in his neighbours' best bed in spurs and oilskins
but not having thrown up:
sprawl is never Calum who, in the loud hallway of our house,
reinvented the Festoon. Rather
it's Beatrice Miles going twelve hundred ditto in a taxi,
No Lewd Advances, No Hitting Animals, No Speeding,
on the proceeds of her two-bob-a-sonnet Shakespeare readings.
An image of my country. And would that it were more so.

No, sprawl is full-gloss murals on a council-house wall.
Sprawl leans on things. It is loose-limbed in its mind.
Reprimanded and dismissed

it listens with a grin and one boot up on the rail
of possibility. It may have to leave the Earth.
Being roughly Christian, it scratches the other cheek
and thinks it unlikely. Though people have been shot for sprawl.

Three Poems in Memory of My Mother,
Miriam Murray née Arnall
Born 23.5.1915, died 19.4.1951

Weights

Not owning a cart, my father
in the drought years was a bowing
green hut of cattle feed, moving,
or gasping under cream cans. No weight
would he let my mother carry.

Instead, she wielded handles
in the kitchen and dairy, singing often,
gave saucepan-boiled injections
with her ward-sister skill, nursed neighbours,
scorned gossips, ran committees.

She gave me her factual tone,
her facial bones, her will,
not her beautiful voice
but her straightness and her clarity.

I did not know back then
nor for many years what it was,
after me, she could not carry.

Midsummer Ice

Remember how I used
to carry ice in from the road
for the ice-chest, half running,
the white rectangle clamped in bare hands
the only utter cold
in all those summer paddocks?

How, swaying, I'd hurry it inside
en bloc and watering, with the butter
and the wrapped bread precarious on top of it?
"Poor Leslie," you would say,
"your hands are cold as charity –"
You made me take the barrow
but uphill it was heavy.

We'd no tongs, and a bag
would have soaked and bumped, off balance.
I loved to eat the ice,
chip it out with the butcher knife's grey steel.
It stopped good things rotting
and it had a strange comb at its heart,
a splintered horizon rife with zero pearls.

But you don't remember.
A doorstep of numbed creek water the colour of tears
but you don't remember.
I will have to die before you remember.

The Steel

I am older than my mother.
Cold steel hurried me from her womb.
I haven't got a star.

What hour I followed
the waters into this world
no one living can now say.
My zodiac got washed away.

The steel of my induction
killed my brothers and sisters;
once or twice I was readied for them

and then they were not mentioned
again, at the hospital
to me or to the visitors.
The reticence left me only.

I think, apart from this,
my parents' life was happy,
provisional, as lives are.

Farming spared them from the war,
that, and an ill-knit blue shin
my father had been harried back

to tree-felling with, by his father
who supervised from horseback.
The times were late pioneer.

So was our bare plank house
with its rain stains down each crack
like tall tan flames,
magic swords, far matched perspectives:

it reaped Dad's shamed invectives –
Paying him rent for this shack!
The landlord was his father.

But we also had fireside ease,
health, plentiful dinners, the radio;
we'd a car to drive to tennis.

Country people have cars
for more than shopping and show,
our Dodge reached voting age, though,
in my first high school year.

I was in the town at school
the afternoon my mother
collapsed, and was carried from the dairy.
The car was out of order.

The ambulance was available
but it took a doctor's say-so
to come. This was refused.
My father pleaded. Was refused.

The local teacher's car was got finally.
The time all this took didn't pass,
it spread through sheets, unstoppable.

Thirty-seven miles to town
and the terrible delay.
Little blood brother, blood sister,
I don't blame you.
How can you blame a baby?
or the longing for a baby?

Little of that week
comes back. The vertigo,
the apparent recovery –
She will get better now.
The relapse on the Thursday.

In school and called away
I was haunted, all that week,
by the spectre of dark women,
Murrays dressed in midday black

who lived on the river islands
and are seen only at funerals;
their terrible weak authority.

Everybody in the town
was asking me about my mother;
I could only answer childishly
to them. And to my mother,

93

and on Friday afternoon
our family world
went inside itself forever.

Sister Arnall, city girl
with your curt good sense
were you being the nurse
when you let them hurry me?
being responsible
when I was brought on to make way
for a difficult birth in that cottage hospital
and the Cheers child stole my birthday?

Or was it our strange diffidence,
unworldly at a pinch, unresentful,
being a case among cases,

a relative, wartime sense,
modern, alien to fuss,
that is not in the Murrays?

I don't blame the Cheers boy's mother:
she didn't put her case.
It was the steel proposed
reasonably, professionally,
that became your sentence

but I don't decry unselfishness:
I'm proud of it. Of you.
Any virtue can be fatal.

In the event, his coming gave no trouble
but it might have, I agree;
nothing you agreed to harmed me.
I didn't mean to harm you
I was a baby.

For a long time, my father
himself became a baby
being perhaps wiser than me,
less modern, less military;

he was not ashamed of grief,
of its looking like a birth
out through the face

bloated, whiskery, bringing no relief.
It was mainly through fear
that I was at times his father.
I have long been sorry.

Caked pans, rancid blankets,
despair and childish cool
were our road to Bohemia
that bitter wartime country.

What were you thinking of,
Doctor MB, BS?
Were you very tired?
Did you have more pressing cases?

Know panic when you heard it:
Oh you can bring her in!
Did you often do
diagnosis by telephone?

Perhaps we wrong you,
make a scapegoat of you;
perhaps there was no stain
of class in your decision,

no view that two framed degrees
outweighed a dairy.
It's nothing, dear:
just some excited hillbilly –

As your practice disappeared
and you were cold-shouldered in town
till you broke and fled,
did you think of the word Clan?

It is an antique
concept. But not wholly romantic.
We came to the river early;
it gives us some protection.

You'll agree the need is real.
I can forgive you now
and not to seem magnanimous.
It's enough that you blundered
on our family steel.

Thirty-five years on earth:
that's short. That's short, Mother,
as the lives cut off by war

and the lives of spilt children are short.
Justice wholly in this world
would bring them no rebirth
nor restore your latter birthdays.
How could that be justice?

My father never quite
remarried. He went back
by stages of kindness to me
to the age of lonely men,
of only men, and men's company

that is called the Pioneer age.
Snig chain and mountain track;
he went back to felling trees
and seeking justice from his
dead father. His only weakness.
One's life is not a case

except of course it is.
Being just, seeking justice:
they were both of them right,
my mother and my father.

There is justice, there is death,
humanist: you can't have both.
Activist, you can't serve both.
You do not move in measured space.

The poor man's anger is a prayer
for equities Time cannot hold
and steel grows from our mother's grace.
Justice is the people's otherworld.

Machine Portraits with Pendant Spaceman
For Valerie

The bulldozer stands short as a boot on its heel-high ripple soles;
it has toecapped stumps aside all day, scuffed earth and trampled
    rocks
making a hobnailed dyke downstream of raw clay shoals.
Its work will hold water. The man who bounced high on the box
seat, exercising levers, would swear a full frontal orthodox
oath to that. First he shaved off the grizzled scrub
with that front-end safety razor supplied by the school of hard
    knocks
then he knuckled down and ground his irons properly; they
    copped many a harsh rub.
At knock-off time, spilling thunder, he surfaced like a sub.

O

Speaking of razors, the workshop amazes with its strop,
its elapsing leather drive-belt angled to the slapstick flow
of fast work in the Chaplin age; tightened, it runs like syrup,
streams like a mill-sluice, fiddles like a glazed virtuoso.

With the straitlaced summary cut of Sam Brownes long ago
it is the last of the drawn lash and bullocking muscle
left in engineering. It's where the panther leaping, his swift
    shadow
and all such free images turned plastic. Here they dwindle, dense
    with oil,
like a skein between tough factory hands, pulley and diesel.

O

Shaking in slow low flight, with its span of many jets,
the combine seeder at nightfall swimming over flat land
is a style of machinery we'd imagined for the fictional planets:
in the high glassed cabin, above vapour-pencilling floodlights,
    a hand,
gloved against the cold, hunts along the medium-wave band
for company of Earth voices; it crosses speech garble music –
the Brandenburg Conch the Who the Illyrian High Command –
as seed wheat in the hoppers shakes down, being laced into the
    thick
night-dampening plains soil, and the stars waver out and stick.

O

Flags and a taut fence discipline the mountain pasture
where giant upturned mushrooms gape mildly at the sky
catching otherworld pollen. Poppy-smooth or waffle-ironed,
    each armature
distils wild and white sound. These, Earth's first antennae
tranquilly angled outwards, to a black, not a gold infinity,
swallow the millionfold numbers that print out as a risen
glorious Apollo. They speak control to satellites in high
bursts of algorithm. And some of them are tuned to win
answers to fair questions, viz. What is the Universe in?

O

How many metal-bra and trumpet-flaring film extravaganzas
underlie the progress of the space shuttle's Ground Transporter

98

Vehicle

across macadam-surfaced Florida? Atop oncreeping house-high
   panzers,

towering drydock and ocean-liner decks, there perches a gridiron
   football

field in gradual motion; it is the god-platform; it sustains the
   bridal

skyscraper of liquid Cool, and the rockets borrowed from the
   Superman

and the bricked aeroplane of Bustout-and-return, all vertical,

conjoined and myth-huge, approaching the starred gantry where
   human

lightning will crack, extend, and vanish upwards from this
   caravan.

O

Gold-masked, the foetal warrior
unslipping on a flawless floor,
I backpack air; my life machine
breathes me head-Earthwards, speaks the Choctaw
of tech-talk that earths our discipline –

but the home world now seems outside-in;
I marvel that here background's so fore
and sheathe my arms in the unseen

a dream in images unrecalled
from any past takes me   I soar
at the heart of fall on a drifting line

this is the nearest I have been
to oneness with the everted world
the unsinking leap   the stone unfurled

O

In a derelict village picture show I will find a projector,
dust-matted, but with film in its drum magazines, and the lens

99

mysteriously clean. The film will be called *Insensate Violence*,
no plot, no characters, just shoot burn scream beg claw
bayonet trample brains – I will hit the reverse switch then, in
    conscience,
and the thing will run backwards, unlike its coeval the machine-
    gun;
blood will unspill, fighters lift and surge apart; horror will be
    undone
and I will come out to a large town, bright parrots round the
    saleyard pens
and my people's faces healed of a bitter sophistication.

O

The more I act, the stiller I become;
the less I'm lit, the more spellbound my crowd;
I accept all colours, and with a warming hum
I turn them white and hide them in a cloud.
To give long life is a power I'm allowed
by my servant, Death. I am what you can't sell
at the world's end – and if you're still beetle-browed
try some of my treasures: an adult bird in its shell
or a pink porker in his own gut, Fritz the Abstract Animal.

O

No riddles about a crane. This one drops a black clanger on cars
and the palm of its four-thumbed steel hand is a raptor of
    wrecked tubing;
the ones up the highway hoist porridgy concrete, long spars
and the local skyline; whether raising aloft on a string
bizarre workaday angels, or letting down a rotating
man on a sphere, these machines are inclined to maintain
a peace like world war, in which we turn over everything
to provide unceasing victories. Now the fluent lines stop, and
    strain
engrosses this tower on the frontier of junk, this crane.

O

Before a landscape sprouts those giant stepladders that pump
    oil
or before far out iron mosquitoes attach to the sea
there is this sortilege with phones that plug into mapped soil,
the odd gelignite bump to shake trucks, paper scribbling out
    serially
as men dial Barrier Reefs long enfolded beneath the geology
or listen for black Freudian beaches; they seek a miles-wide
    pustular
rock dome of pure Crude, a St Paul's-in-profundis. There are
    many
wrong numbers on the geophone, but it's brought us some
    distance, and by car.
Every machine has been love and a true answer.

O

Not a high studded ship boiling cauliflower under her keel
nor a ghost in bootlaced canvas – just a length of country road
afloat between two shores, winding wet rope reel-to-reel,
dismissing romance sternwards. Six cars and a hay truck are her
    load
plus a thoughtful human cast which could, in some dramatic
    episode,
become a world. All machines in the end join God's creation
growing bygone, given, changeless – but a river ferry has its
    timeless mode
from the grinding reedy outset; it enforces contemplation.
We arrive. We traverse depth in thudding silence. We go on.

The Hypogeum

Below the moveable gardens of this shopping centre
down concrete ways
                    to a level of rainwater,

a black lake glimmering among piers, electric lighted,
windless, of no depth.
                    Rare shafts of daylight
waver at their base. As the water is shaken, the few
cars parked down here seem to rock. In everything
their strains that silent crash, that reverberation
which persists in concrete.
                    The cardboard carton
Lorenzo's Natural Flavour Italian Meat Balls has foundered
into a wet ruin. Dutch Cleanser is propped at a high
featureless wall. Self-Raising Flour is still floating
and supermarket trolleys hang their inverse harps,
silver leaking from them.
                    What will help the informally religious
to endure peace?: Surface water dripping into
this underworld makes now a musical blip,
now rings from nowhere.
                    Young people descending the ramp
pause at the water's brink, banging their voices.

An Immortal

Beckoner of hotheads, brag-tester, lord of the demi-suicides,
in only one way since far before Homer have you altered:
when now, on wry wheels still revolving, the tall dust showers
        back
and tongue-numbing Death stills a screaming among the jagged
        images,
you disdain to strip your victims' costly armour, bright with fire
        and duco
or even to step forth, visible briefly in your delusive harness,
glass cubes whirling at your tread, the kinked spear of frenzy in
        your hand.

Do you appear, though, bodily to your vanquished challengers
with the bare face of the boy who was large and quickest at it,
the hard face of the boss and the bookie, strangely run together,

the face of the expert craftsman, smiling privately, shaking his
    head?
Are you sometimes the Beloved, approaching and receding
    through the glaze?
Or is this all merely cinema? Are your final interviews wholly
    personal
and the bolt eyes disjunct teeth blood-vomit all a kind mask lent
    by physics?

We will never find out, living. The volunteers, wavering and
    firm,
and the many conscripted to storm the house of meaning
have stayed inside, with the music. Or else they are ourselves,
sheepish, reminiscent, unsure how we made it past the Warrior
into our lives – which the glory of his wheeled blade has infected
so that, on vacant evenings, we may burn with the mystery of
    his face,
his speed, his streetlights pointing every way, his unbelief in
    joking.

Second Essay on Interest: the Emu

Weathered blond as a grass tree, a huge Beatles haircut
raises an alert periscope and stares out
over scrub. Her large olivine eggs click
oilily together; her lips of noble plastic
clamped in their expression, her head-fluff a stripe
worn mohawk style, she bubbles her pale-blue windpipe:
the emu, *Dromaius novaehollandiae*,
whose stand-in on most continents is an antelope,
looks us in both eyes with her one eye
and her other eye, dignified courageous hump,
feather-swaying condensed camel, Swift Courser of New
    Holland.

Knees backward in toothed three-way boots, you stand,
Dinewan, proud emu, common as the dust
in your sleeveless cloak, returning our interest.
Your shield of fashion's wobbly: you're Quaint, you're Native,
even somewhat Bygone. You may be let live
but beware: the blank zones of Serious disdain
are often carte blanche to the darkly human.
Europe's boats on their first strange shore looked humble
but, Mass over, men started renaming the creatures.
Worship turned to interest and had new features.
Now only life survives, if it's made remarkable.

Heraldic bird, our protection is a fable
made of space and neglect. We're remarkable and not;
we're the ordinary discovered on a strange planet.
Are you Early or Late, in the history of birds
which doesn't exist, and is deeply ancient?
My kinships, too, are immemorial and recent,
like my country, which abstracts yours in words.
This distillate of mountains is finely branched, this plain
expanse of dour delicate lives, where the rain,
shrouded slab on the west horizon, is a corrugated revenant
settling its long clay-tipped plumage in a hatching descent.

Rubberneck, stepped sister, I see your eye on our jeep's load.
I think your story is, when you were offered
the hand of evolution, you gulped it. Forefinger and thumb
project from your face, but the weighing palm is inside you
collecting the bottletops, nails, wet cement that you famously
    swallow,
your passing muffled show, your serially private museum.
Some truths are now called *trivial*, though. Only God approves
    them.
Some humans who disdain them make a kind of weather
which, when it grows overt and widespread, we call *war*.
There we make death trivial and awesome, by rapid turns about,
we conscript it to bless us, force-feed it to squeeze the drama
    out;

indeed we imprison and torture death – this part is called *peace* –
we offer it murder like mendicants, begging for significance.
You rustle dreams of pardon, not fleeing in your hovercraft style,
not gliding fast with zinc-flaked legs dangling, feet making high-
    tensile
seesawing impacts. Wasteland parent, barely edible dignitary,
the disinterested spotlight of the lords of interest
and gowned nobles of ennui is a torch of vivid arrest
and blinding after-darkness. But you hint it's a brigand sovereignty
after the steady extents of God's common immortality
whose image is daylight detail, aggregate, in process yet plumb
to the everywhere focus of one devoid of boredom.

A Retrospect of Humidity

All the air conditioners now slacken
their hummed carrier wave. Once again
we've served our three months with remissions
in the steam and dry iron of this seaboard.
In jellied glare, through the nettle-rash season
we've watched the sky's fermenting laundry
portend downpours. Some came, and steamed away,
and we were clutched back into the rancid
saline midnights of orifice weather,
to damp grittiness and wiping off the air.

Metaphors slump irritably together in
the muggy weeks. Shark and jellyfish shallows
become suburbs where you breathe a fat towel;
babies burst like tomatoes with discomfort
in the cotton-wrapped pointing street markets;
the Lycra-bulging surf drips from non-swimmers
miles from shore, and somehow includes soil.
Skins, touching, soak each other. Skin touching
any surface wets that and itself
in a kind of mutual digestion.
Throbbing heads grow lianas of nonsense.

It's our annual visit to the latitudes
of rice, kerosene and resignation,
an averted, temporary visit
unrelated, for most, to the attitudes
of festive northbound jets gaining height –
closer, for some few, to the memory
of ulcers scraped with a tin spoon
or sweated faces bowing before dry
where the flesh is worn inside out,
all the hunger-organs clutched in rank nylon,
by those for whom exhaustion is spirit:

an intrusive, heart-narrowing season
at this far southern foot of the monsoon.
As the kleenex flower, the hibiscus
drops its browning wads, we forget
annually, as one forgets a sickness.
The stifling days will never come again,
not now that we've seen the first sweater
tugged down on the beauties of division
and inside the rain's millions, a risen
loaf of cat on a cool night verandah.

Flowering Eucalypt in Autumn

That slim creek out of the sky
the dried-blood western gum tree
is all stir in its high reaches:

its strung haze-blue foliage is dancing
points down in breezy mobs, swapping
pace and place in an all-over sway

retarded en masse by crimson blossom.
Bees still at work up there tack
around their exploded furry likeness

and the lawn underneath's a napped rug
of eyelash drift, of blooms flared
like a sneeze in a redhaired nostril,

minute urns, pinch-sized rockets
knocked down by winds, by night-creaking
fig-squirting bats, or the daily

parrot gang with green pocketknife wings.
Bristling food for tough delicate
raucous life, each flower comes

as a spray in its own turned vase,
a taut starburst, honeyed model
of the tree's fragrance crisping in your head.

When the Japanese plum tree
was shedding in spring, we speculated
there among the drizzling petals

what kind of exquisitely precious
artistic bloom might be gendered
in a pure ethereal compost

of petals potted as they fell.
From unpetalled gum-debris
we know what is grown continually,

a tower of fabulous swish tatters,
a map hoisted upright, a crusted
riverbed with up-country show towns.

The Smell of Coal Smoke

John Brown, glowing far and down,
wartime Newcastle was a brown town,
handrolled cough and cardigan, rain on paving bricks,
big smoke to a four-year-old from the green sticks.
Train city, mother's city, coming on dark,
Japanese shell holes awesome in a park,
electric light and upstairs, encountered first that day,
sailors and funny ladies in Jerry's Fish Café.

It is always evening on those earliest trips,
raining through the tram wires where blue glare rips
across the gaze of wonderment and leaves thrilling tips.
The steelworks' vast roofed débris unrolling falls
of smoky stunning orange, its eye-hurting slump walls
mellow to lounge interiors, cut pile and curry-brown
with the Pears-Soap-smelling fire and a sense of ships
mourning to each other below in the town.

This was my mother's childhood and her difference,
her city-brisk relations who valued Sense
talking strike and colliery, engineering, fowls and war,
Brown's grit and miners breathing it, years before
as I sat near the fire, raptly touching coal,
its blockage, slick yet dusty, prisms massed and dense
in the iron scuttle, its hammered bulky roll
into the glaring grate to fracture and shoal,

its chips you couldn't draw with on the cement
made it a stone, tar crockery, different –
and I had three grandparents, while others had four:
where was my mother's father, never called Poor?
In his tie and his Vauxhall that had a boat bow
driving up the Coalfields, but where was he now?
Coal smoke as much as gum trees now had a tight scent
to summon deep brown evenings of the Japanese war,

to conjure gaslit pub yards, their razory frisson
and sense my dead grandfather, the Grafton Cornishman
rising through the night schools by the pressure in his chest
as his lungs creaked like mahogany with the grains of John Brown.
His city, mother's city, at its starriest
as swearing men with doctors' bags streamed by towards the
    docks
past the smoke-frothing wooden train that would take us home
    soon
with our day-old Henholme chickens peeping in their box.

The Mouthless Image of God in the Hunter-Colo Mountains

Starting a dog, in the past-midnight suburbs, for a laugh,
barking for a lark, or to nark and miff, being tough
or dumbly meditative, starting gruff, sparking one dog off
almost companionably, you work him up, playing the rough riff
of punkish mischief, get funky as a poultry-farm diff
and vary with the Prussian note: *Achtung! Schar, Gewehr' auf!*
starting all the dogs off, for the tinny chain reaction and stiff
far-spreading music, the backyard territorial guff
echoing off brick streets, garbage cans, off every sandstone cliff
in miles-wide canine circles, a vast haze of auditory stuff
with every dog augmenting it, tail up, mouth serrated, shoulder
    ruff
pulsing with its outputs, a continuous clipped yap from a hand-
    muff
Pomeranian, a labrador's ascending fours, a Dane grown great
    enough
to bark in the singular, many raffish bitzers blowing their gaff
as humans raise windows and cries and here and there the roof
and you barking at the epicentre, you, putting a warp to the
    woof,
shift the design with a throat-rubbing lull and ill howl,
dingo-vibrant, not shrill, which starts a howling school

among hill-and-hollow barkers, till horizons-wide again a tall
pavilion of mixed timbres is lifted up eerily in full call
and the wailing takes a toll: you, from playing the fool
move, behind your arch will, into the sorrow of a people.

O

And not just one people. You've entered a sound-proletariat
where pigs exclaim *boff-boff!* making off in fright
and fowls say *chirk* in tiny voices when a snake's about,
quite unlike the rooster's *Chook Chook*, meaning look, a good bit:
hens, get stoock into it! Where the urgent boar mutters *root-root*
to his small harassed sow, trotting back and forth beside her,
   rut-rut
and the she-cat's curdling *Mao*? where are kittens? mutating to
   prr-mao,
come along, kittens, quite different words from *prr-au*,
general-welcome-and-acceptance, or extremity's portmanteau
   mee-EU!
Active and passive at once, the boar and feeding sow
share a common prone *unh*, expressing repletion and bestowing
   it,
and you're where the staid dog, excited, emits a mouth-skirl
he was trying to control, and looks ashamed of it
and the hawk above the land calls himself Peter P. P. Pew,
where, far from class hatred, the rooster scratches up some for
   you
and edgy plovers sharpen their nerves on a blurring wheel.
Waterbirds address you in their neck-flexure language, hiss and
   bow
and you speak to each species in the seven or eight
planetary words of its language, which ignore and include the
   detail
God set you to elaborate by the dictionary-full
when, because they would reveal their every secret,
He took definition from the beasts and gave it to you.

If at baying time you have bayed with dogs and not humans
you know enough not to scorn the moister dimensions
of language, nor to build on the sandbanks of Dry.
You long to show someone non-human the diaphragm-shuffle
which may be your species' only distinctive cry,
the spasm which, in various rhythms, turns our face awry,
contorts speech, shakes the body, and makes our eyelids liquefy.
Approaching adulthood, one half of this makes us shy
and the other's a touchy spear-haft we wield for balance.
Laughter-and-weeping. It's the great term the small terms qualify
as a whale is qualified by all the near glitters of the sea.
Weightless leviathan our showering words overlie and modify,
it rises irresistibly. All our dry-eyed investigations
supply that one term, in the end; its occasions multiply,
the logics issue in horror, we are shattered by joy
till the old prime divider bends and its two ends unify
and the learned words bubble off us. We laugh because we cry:
the crying depth of life is too great not to laugh
but laugh or cry singly aren't it: only mingled are they spirit
to wobble and sing us as a summer dawn sings a magpie.
For spirit is the round earth bringing our flat earth to bay
and we're feasted and mortified, exposed to those momentary
        heavens
which, speaking in speech on the level, we work for and deny.

Time Travel

To revisit the spitfire world
of the duel, you put on a suit
of white body armour, a helmet
like an insect's composite eye
and step out like a space walker
under haloed lights, trailing a cord.

Descending, with nodding foil in hand
towards the pomander-and-cravat sphere
you meet the Opponent, for this journey
can only be accomplished by a pair
who semaphore and swap quick respect
before they set about their joint effect

which is making zeroes and serifs so
swiftly and with such sprung variety
that the long steels skid, clatter, zing,
switch, batter, bite, kiss and ring
in the complex rhythms of that society
with its warrior snare of comme il faut

that has you facing a starched beau
near stable walls on a misty morning,
striking, seeking the surrender in him,
the pedigree-flaw through which to pin him,
he probing for your own braggadocio,
confusion, ennui or inner fawning –

Seconds, holding stakes and cloths, look grim
and surge a step. Exchanges halt
for one of you stands, ageing horribly,
collapses, drowning from an entry
of narrow hurt. The other gulps hot chocolate
a trifle fast, but talking nonchalant –

a buzzer sounds. Heads are tucked
under arms, and you and he swap
curt nods in a more Christian century.

Three Interiors

The mansard roof of the Barrier Industrial Council's
pale-blue Second Empire building in Broken Hill
announces the form of a sprightly, intricately painted
pressed metal ceiling, spaciously stepped and tie-beamed

high over the main meeting hall. The factual light
of the vast room is altered, in its dusty rising
toward that coloured mime of myriadness, that figured
carpet of the mind, whose marvel comes down the clean walls
almost to the shoulder-stain level, the rubbings of mass defiance
which circle the hall miner-high above worn-out timber flooring.
Beauty all suspended in air – I write from memory
but it was so when we were there. A consistent splendour,
quite abstract, bloc-voted, crystalline with colour junctions
and regulated tendrils, high in its applied symphonic theory
above the projection hatch, over sports gear and the odd steel
    chair
marooned on the splintery extents of the former dance floor.

The softly vaulted ceiling of St Gallen's monastic library
is beautifully iced in Rococo butter cream with scrolled pipework
surf-dense around islands holding russet-clad, vaguely heavenly
personages who've swum up from the serried volumes below.
The books themselves, that vertical live leather brickwork
in the violin-curved, gleaming bays, have all turned their backs
on the casual tourist and, clasped in meditation, they pray
in coined Greek, canonical Latin, pointed Hebrew.
It is an utterly quiet pre-industrial machine room
on a submarine to Heaven, and the deck, the famous floor
over which you pad in blanket slippers, has flowed in
honey-lucent around the footings, settled suavely level and
    hardened:
only the winding darker woods and underwater star-points
of the parquetry belie that impression. What is below
resembles what's above, but just enough, as cloud-shadow,
runways and old lake shores half noticed in mellow wheat
    land.

The last interior is darkness. Befuddled past-midnight
fear, testing each step like deep water, that when you open
the eventual refrigerator, cold but no light will envelop you.
Bony hurts that persuade you the names of your guides now
are balance, and gravity. You can fall up things, but not far.
A stopping, teeming caution. As of prey. The dark is arbitrary

delivering wheeled smashes, murmurings, something that
    scuttled,
doorjambs without a switch. The dark has no subject matter
but is alive with theory. Its best respites are: no surprises.
Nothing touching you. Or panic-stilling chance embraces.
Darkness is the cloth for pained eyes, and lovely in colour,
splendid in the lungs of great singers. Also the needed matrix
of constellations, flaring Ginzas, desert moons, apparent snow,
verandah-edged night rain. Dark is like that: all productions.
Almost nothing there is caused, or has results. Dark is all one
    interior
permitting only inner life. Concealing what will seize it.

Morse

Tuckett. Bill Tuckett. Telegraph operator, Hall's Creek
which is way out back of the Outback, but he stuck it,
quite likely liked it, despite heat, glare, dust and the lack
of diversion or doctors. Come disaster you trusted to luck,
ingenuity and pluck. This was back when nice people said pluck,
the sleevelink and green eyeshade epoch.
                            Faced, though, like Bill Tuckett
with a man needing surgery right on the spot, a lot
would have done their dashes. It looked hopeless (dot dot dot)
Lift him up on the table, said Tuckett, running the key hot
till Head Office turned up a doctor who coolly instructed
up a thousand miles of wire, as Tuckett advanced slit by slit
with a safety razor blade, pioneering on into the wet,
copper-wiring the rivers off, in the first operation conducted
along dotted lines, with rum drinkers gripping the patient:
d-d-dash it, take care, Tuck!
                            And the vital spark stayed unshorted.
Yallah! breathed the camelmen. Tuckett, you did it, you did it!
cried the spattered la-de-dah jodhpur-wearing Inspector of Stock.
We imagine, some weeks later, a properly laconic
convalescent averring Without you, I'd have kicked the bucket...

From Chungking to Burrenjuck, morse keys have mostly gone
    silent
and only old men meet now to chit-chat in their electric
bygone dialect. The last letter many will forget
is dit-dit-dit-dah, V for Victory. The coders' hero had speed,
resource and a touch. So ditd:tdit daah for Bill Tuckett.

Late Snow in Edinburgh

Snow on the day before Anzac! ⸑
A lamb-killing wind out of Ayr
heaped a cloud up on towering Edinburgh
in the night, and left it adhering
to parks and leafing trees in the morning,
a cloud decaying on the upper city,
on the stepped medieval skyscrapers there,
cassata broadcast on the lower city
to be a hiss on buzzing cobblestones
under soaped cars, and cars still shaving.

All day the multiplying whiteness
persisted, now dazzling, now resumed
into the spectral Northern weather,
moist curd out along the Castle clifftops,
linen collar on the Mound, pristine pickings
in the Cowgate's blackened teeth, deposits
in Sir Walter Scott's worked tusk, and under
the soaked blue banners walling Princes Street.
The lunchtime gun fired across dun distances
ragged with keen tents. By afternoon, though,
derelicts sleeping immaculate in wynds
and black areas had shrivelled to wet sheep.
Froth, fading, stretched thinner on allotments.

115

As the melting air browned into evening
the photographed city, in last umber
and misty first lights, was turning into
the stones in a vast furrow. For that moment
half a million moved in an earth cloud
harrowed up, damp and fuming, seeded
with starry points, with luminous still patches
that wouldn't last the night. No Anzac Day
prodigies for the visitor-descendant.
The snow was dimming into Spring's old
Flanders jacket and frieze trousers. Hughie Spring,
the droll ploughman, up from the Borders.

Art History: The Suburb of Surrealls

We dreamed very wide awake
those days, for obedience's sake:

In the suburb of Surrealls
horse families board the airline bus
to sell packages of phlegm.
My notebook is hugely swollen.
For some reason I am American.

Such dreaming is enforceable.
Everyone became guarded;
a tinkling of symbols was heard.
It's the West occupying the dreamworld
because the East has captured reason,
some said. Many ceased to listen.

In fact we'd gone to the dream
for supplies of that instant
paint of the twilight kingdom
which colours every object
supernal, deeply important.
Spirit-surrogate. We even synthesised it.

Exposed to the common air, it
weathered quickly to the tone
of affectless weird despair,
elegant barely contained anger
our new patrons demanded
when we had trained them to it.

False dreamings are imperial
but we couldn't disappoint them
(Few others now read us by choice.
Woolf! Woolf! our master's voice).

To be fair, many of us
had now joined the creative class
and become our masters
– but the paint, when stolen
and breathed straight from the tin
gave a noble deathly rush
that ensnared imagination.

Satis Passio

Elites, levels, proletariat:
the uniting cloth crowns
of Upper and Lower Egypt
suggest theories of poetry
which kindness would accept
to bestow, like Heaven, dignity
on the inept and the ept,
one Papuan warrior's phallocrypt
the soaring equal of its fellowcrypt.

By these measures, most knowledge
in our heads is poetry,
varied crystals of detail, chosen
by dream-interest, and poured spirally
from version to myth, with spillage,

from theory to history
and, with toppings-up, to story,
not metered, lined or free
but condensed by memory
to roughly vivid essences:
most people's poetry is now this.
Some of it is made by poets.

God bless the feral poetries,
littératures and sensibilities,
theory, wonder, the human gamut
leaping cheerfully or in heavy earnest
– but there is this quality to art
which starts, rather than ends, at the gist.
Not the angle, but the angel.

Art is what can't be summarised:
it has joined creation from our side,
entered Nature, become a fact
and acquired presence,
more like ourselves or any subject
swirled around, about, in and out,
than like the swirling poetries.

Art's best is a standing miracle
at an uncrossable slight distance,
an anomaly, finite but inexhaustible,
unaltered after analysis
as an ancient face.

Not the portrait of one gone
merely, no pathos of the bygone
but a section, of all that exist,
a passage, a whole pattern
that has shifted the immeasurable
first step into Heaven.
A first approximation.
Where is heaven? Down these roads.

The fine movement of art's face
before us is a motionless traffic
between here and remote Heaven.
It is out through this surface,
we may call it the Unfalling Arrow,
this third mode, and perhaps by art first
that there came to us the dream-plan
of equality and justice,
long delayed by the poetries –

but who was the more numinous,
Pharaoh or the hunted Nile heron?
more splendid, the iris or Solomon?
Beauty lives easily with equities
more terrible than theory dares mean.
Of the workers set free to break stone
and the new-cracked stone, which is more luminous?

God bless the general poetries?
This is how it's done.

Federation Style on the Northern Rivers

And entering on the only smooth road
this steamer glides past the rattling shipyard
where they're having the usual Aboriginal
whale-feast in reverse, with scaffolding and planking;
engine smoke marching through blue sheoak trees
along the edge of Jack Robertson farms,
the river opens and continually opens

and lashed on deck, a Vauxhall car
intricate in brass, with bonnet grooves,
a bulb to squawk, great guillotine levers,
high diamond-buttoned leather club chairs

and dressing-table windscreen to flash afar:
in British cherry metal, detailed in mustard
it cruises up country with a moveless wheel.

In the town it approaches, a Habsburg-yellow store
Provisions – Novelties – J. Cornwell Prop.
contains a knot of debt that has reached
straining point, tugging between many poor
selector farmers and several not necessarily
rich city suppliers. Mobilised, it can tear
the store apart, uproot many families

and tomorrow the auditor will be in town
and the car will be parked just where he comes
after a prolonged hilarious midday dinner
I see your town's acquired a motor –
You fancy those beasts, do you, Stickney?
One face grows inspired, in step with the other.
What is that sly joker Cornwell at?

asks the Bank of Australasia's swank bow window:
How can he have afforded a motor?
but a schooner bee deflects the questioner.
Would you like to take a spin in her,
Stickney? – I daresay your books will wait
for half an hour . . . One mounts from the left,
one hoists the crankhandle. Directly, indirectly

they wind down the street over horsemanures
of varying fatness, past the Coffee Palace
unconcerned with ales – *Stickney, you're a marvel!*
Just aim her straight and don't shout Whoa!
Tread on that to slow her: don't tug the wheel –
Children running, neighbours cheering, *Go it, Jim!*
Mr Cornwell lifts his hat to the faces greeting him.

Smashing water-windows along the parallel
wheeltracks of the cart-cut river road
they pass the deeply-laden Cornwell shop-boat

Turn inland here: we will have drier going.
I agree she'd be a buy, Stickney: I'd have to think –
Think how to waste more afternoon
with the tall affection of local tales:

...And old Tom Beattie managing himself
along, like a bad horse; you hear him curse it:
Hold up, you bugger! Walk – Mr Cornwell,
we should get back, to your ledgers. – Yes.
Take the left fork two miles on. A shortcut –
The shortcut ends in blackpudding bog
and no country curricles bowling by it.

Dear God, Cornwell, I must catch tomorrow's boat!
but heaving, corduroying, pole-levering all fail
and Cornwell must vanish through the rung timber.
For Stickney there will now accrue a wait
heavy as blacksoil around buried wheels.
Shanks' pony? Not I. Not through snaky bush.
He watches a swamp pheasant's sailing flight

and on the creekbank, in a place where cattle,
the white man's firesticks, can't come
he finds a child's small bowerbird farm:
scraped roads, wharf, little twig cattleyards,
clay beasts. A new world, already immemorial.
He will tighten his coat against evening chill
long before Cornwell reappears with helpers.

That night the yellow store will burn
in a jammed eye-parching abolishment of proof
and the car, strangely spotless, will not be harmed.
Tomorrow the innocent owner will collect it.
The steamer hoots. *Cornwell, now that you're*
safely ruined: where did you go yesterday?
– I had to dodge certain bandicoot farms

where the little ones bolt up under the house
at the sight of a stranger, I've never cared

121

to be a stranger who threatens children.
They part, across water, with the ghost of a salute.
Certain surnames will now survive in the district.
As the town declines through the mulberry years
Cornwell will receive odd grateful sovereigns.
The rebuilt store will be kept by a Hogan.

Easter 1984

When we saw human dignity
healing humans in the middle of the day

we moved in on him slowly
under the incalculable gravity

of old freedom, of our own freedom,
under atmospheres of consequence, of justice

under which no one needs to thank anyone.
If this was God, we would get even.

And in the end we nailed him,
lashed, spittled, stretched him limb from limb.

We would settle with dignity
for the anguish it had caused us,

we'd send it to be abstract again,
we would set it free.

O

But we had raised up evolution.
It would not stop being human.

Ever afterwards, the accumulation
of freedom would end in this man

whipped, bloodied, getting the treatment.
It would look like man himself getting it.

He was freeing us, painfully, of freedom,
justice, dignity – he was discharging them

of their deadly ambiguous deposit,
remaking out of them the primal day

in which he was free not to have borne it
and we were free not to have done it,

free never to torture man again,
free to believe him risen.

O

Remember the day when life increased,
explainably or outright, was haloed in poignancy,

straight life, given not attained, unlurching ecstasy,
arrest of the guards for once, and ourself released,

splendour taking detail, beyond the laughter-and-tears
if those were gateway to it, a still or moving utterness

in and all around us. Four have been this human
night and day, steadily. Three fell, two went on.

A laser of this would stand the litter-bound or Lazarus
upright, stammering, or unshroud absent Jesus

whose anguish was to be for a whole day lost to this,
making of himself the companionway of our species

up from where such love is an unreal, half-forgotten
peak, and not the baseline of the human.

Physiognomy on the Savage Manning River

Walking on that early shore, in our bodies,
the autumn ocean has become wasp-waisted:
a scraped timber mansion hung in showering
ropework is crabbing on the tide's flood,
swarming, sway, and shouting,
entering the rivermouth over the speedy bar.

As it calms into the river, the Tahitian
helmsman, a pipe-smoking archer,
draws and tightens the wheel. The spruce captain
meanwhile celebrates the bohême of revolutions
with a paper cigarette, and the carpenter,
deepwater man, combs his sulky boy's hair.

Seo abhainn mar loch – the polished river is indeed
like a loch, without flow, clear to the rainforest islands
and the Highland immigrants on deck, remarking it
keep a hand, or a foot, on their bundles and nail-kegs.
No equipment is replaceable: there's only one of anything,
experience they will hand down.

Beyond the river brush extends the deserted
aboriginal hunting park. There is far less blue
out in the grassland khaki than in our lifetime
though the hills are darkening, sprinkling outward,
closing on crusted lagoons. Nowhere a direct line;
no willows yet, nor any houses.
Those are in the low hills upriver.
Beyond are the ranges, edge over edge, like jumbled sabres.

Crocodile chutes slant out of the riverbank forest
where great logs have been launched.
It is the feared long-unburnable
dense forest of the doolgarl. The cannibal solitary
humanoid of no tribe. Here, as worldwide, he and she
are hairy, nightmare-agile, with atavisms of the feet.
Horror can be ascribed and strange commissions given
to the fireless doolgarl. Killer, here, of gingery bat-hunters.

Tiptoeing after its slung leadline, the ship moves forward
for hours into the day. Raising the first dogleg paddocks,
the first houses, the primal blowflies.
Soup and clothing
boil in a fire-hut, in cauldrons slung on steel saws
there where next century's pelicans will haunt the Fish
        Cooperative.

The gossip on the river is all Miss Isabella Kelly:
triumphing home with her libel case now won
and, for her months in gaol, a thousand pounds compensation
she has found her stations devastated:
yards smashed, homestead burnt, cattle lifted
(irrecoverable nods are winked here).
Now she has sailed to England in her habitual infuriated self
        esteem.
She will have Charles Dickens write her story.
Voices, calling God to forgive them, wish her drowned.

Isabella Mary Kelly. The shadowy first landholder.
Now she has given the district a larger name
to drop than her own. She, who rode beside
her walking convicts three days through the wilderness
to have them flogged half-insane in proper form
at Port Macquarie and Raymond Terrace
then walked them immediately back,
who told the man who dragged her from swift floodwater
"You waste your gallantry. You are still due a lashing.
Walk on, croppy."

Isabella Kelly, of the sidesaddle acerbities,
grazier and pistol shot
throned and footless in her hooped midcentury skirts,
for some years it has been she,
and perhaps it really was she, who mixed the deadly crystals
with the natives' flour ration at Belbora,
Miss Kelly all alone. The colonies' earlier Kelly.
Jilted in Dublin – or is that an acanthus leaf
of motivation, modelled over something barer?

Suddenly her time has passed.
Death in a single room in chilly Sydney
still lies ahead – and being confused with Kate Kelly –
but she has moved already into her useful legend.

Now up every side creek a youth in a cabbagetree hat
is rocking like a steersman, feinting like a boxer:
every stone of gravel must go a round or two
in a circling dish, and the pouring of waters be adjusted.
The same on every track round the heads of rivers:
men escaping the black mills
and families tired of a thousand years' dim tenancy
are entering the valley beside their jolting stacks;
there is even the odd spanker
reins in hand behind trotters, on a seat like a chocolate éclair,
though he is as yet rare;
more are riding through horse-high grass, and into timber
that thickens, like work, to meet their mighty need of it.

The ship is tied up meanwhile in a sort
of farmyard dockland:
pigs under the wharf, saddles, pumpkin patches, corn boats.
The men unloading her, who never doff their shirts
are making whips of tin;
this one who has worn the white clay girdle of the Bora,
of sung rebirth, now plies a lading hook
to keep his Kentish wife.
At spell-oh time, they will share a pipe of tobacco
which she has shaved from the succulent twist with her case-
      knife.

Farther up-river, men are rolling out on to their wharf
big solid barrels of a mealy wetness
and others with axes are dismembering downed cattle
in jarring sight of yarded herds. They heave the pieces
into huge smoking trypots. It is the boiling-down,
a kind of inland sealing.
The boiled-out meat is pitched down a cloacal gully.

All that can be exported of the squatters' cattle
of the spinster Kelly's cattle and the others'
is their tallow, for candles.
Lights for the sickroom, lustre for pianoforte sconces.
Cattle distilled to a fluted wax, and sea creatures
sublimated to a liquor light the readers
of Charles Darwin and Charles Dickens.
On sleeping skins, snorting boys drip melted cattle.

Now the gently wrecking cornfields relax, and issue
parents and children. What do families offer us?
Some protection from history,
a tough school of forgiveness.
After the ship has twitched minutely out of
focus and back, as many times as there were barrels
and night has assumed the slab huts and sawn houses
the faces drinking tea by their various lights
include some we had thought modern. The mask of unappeasable
rage is there, and those of scorn's foundling aristocracy,
among the timeless sad and contented faces,
the vacant and remote faces. Only the relative
licensing of expressions is wholly different.
Blame is not yet privileged.

And, walking on that early shore in our bodies
(perhaps the only uncowardly way to do history)
if we asked leading questions, we might hear,
short of a ringing ear,
something like: We do what's to be done
and some things because we can.
Don't be taking talk out of me.

Such not only from the haughtily dreaming,
intelligent, remorseless, secretly amused still face
of Isabella Kelly.
As the Highlandman said
eating his first meal of fresh beef and cornmeal porridge
after landing today:
Thig lá choin duibh fhathast. The black dog will have his day yet.
Not every dog, as in English, but the black dog.

127

The Dream of Wearing Shorts Forever

To go home and wear shorts forever
in the enormous paddocks, in that warm climate,
adding a sweater when winter soaks the grass,

to camp out along the river bends
for good, wearing shorts, with a pocketknife,
a fishing line and matches,

or there where the hills are all down, below the plain,
to sit around in shorts at evening
on the plank verandah –

If the cardinal points of costume
are Robes, Tato, Rig and Scunge,
where are shorts in this compass?

They are never Robes
as other bareleg outfits have been:
the toga, the kilt, the lava-lava,
the Mahatma's cotton dhoti;

archbishops and field marshals
at their ceremonies never wear shorts.
The very word
means underpants in North America.

Shorts can be Tat,
Land-Rovering, bush-environmental tat,
socio-political ripped-and-metal-stapled tat,
solidarity-with-the-Third World tat tvam asi,

likewise track-and-field shorts worn to parties
and the further humid, modelling negligée
of the Kingdom of Flaunt,
that unchallenged aristocracy.

More plainly climatic, shorts
are farmers' rig, leathery with salt and bonemeal,
are sailors' and branch bankers' rig,
the crisp golfing style
of our youngest male National Costume.

Most loosely, they are Scunge,
ancient Bengal bloomers or moth-eaten hot pants
worn with a former shirt,
feet, beach sand, hair
and a paucity of signals.

Scunge, which is real negligée,
housework in a swimsuit, pyjamas worn all day,
is holiday, is freedom from ambition.
Scunge makes you invisible
to the world and yourself.

The entropy of costume,
scunge can get you conquered by more vigorous cultures
and help you to notice it less.

To be or to become
is a serious question posed by a work-shorts counter
with its pressed stacks, bulk khaki and blue,
reading Yakka or King Gee, crisp with steely warehouse odour.

Satisfied ambition, defeat, true unconcern,
the wish and the knack for self-forgetfulness
all fall within the scunge ambit
wearing board shorts or similar;
it is a kind of weightlessness.

Unlike public nakedness, which in Westerners
is deeply circumstantial, relaxed as exam time,
artless and equal as the corsetry of a hussar regiment,

shorts and their plain like
are an angelic nudity,
spirituality with pockets!
A double updraft as you drop from branch to pool!

Ideal for getting served last
in shops of the temperate zone
they are also ideal for going home, into space,
into time, to farm the mind's Sabine acres
for product or subsistence.

– Now that everyone who yearned to wear long pants
has essentially achieved them,
long pants, which have themselves been underwear
repeatedly, and underground more than once,
it is time perhaps to cherish the culture of shorts,

to moderate grim vigour
with the knobble of bare knees,
to cool bareknuckle feet in inland water,
slapping flies with a book on solar wind
or a patient bare hand, beneath the cadjiput trees,

to be walking meditatively
among green timber, through the grassy forest
towards a calm sea
and looking across to more of that great island
and the further tropics.

The Aquatic Carnival

Two racing boats seen from the harmonic railing
of this road bridge quit their wakes,
plane above their mirroring shield-forms
and bash the river, flat out, their hits batts of appliqué

violently spreading, their turnings eiderdown
abolishing translucency before the frieze of people,
and rolled-over water comes out to the footings of the carnival.

Even up drinking coffee-and-froth in the town
prodigious sound rams through arcades and alleyways
and burrs in our teeth, beneath the slow nacelle
of a midsummer ceiling fan.
No wonder pelicans vanish from their river at these times.
How, we wonder, does that sodden undersized one
who hangs around the Fish Co-op get by?
The pert wrymouth with the twisted upper beak.

It cannot pincer prey, or lid its lower scoop
and so lives on guts, mucking in with the others
who come and go. For it to leave would be death.
Its trouble looks like a birth defect, not an injury
and raises questions.
There are poetics would require it to be pecked
to death by fellow pelicans, or kids to smash it with a stick,
preserving a hard cosmos.

In fact it came with fellow pelicans, parents maybe
and has been around for years. Humans who feed it
are sentimental perhaps – but what to say
of humans who refused to feed a lame bird?
Nature is not human-hearted. But it is one flesh
or we could not imagine it. And we could not eat.

Nature is not human-hearted. So the animals
come to man, at first in their extremity:
the wild scrub turkeys entering farms in drought-time,
the done fox suddenly underfoot among dog-urgers
(that frantic compliment, that prayer never granted by dogs)
or the shy birds perching on human shoulders and trucks
when the mountains are blotted out in godly dismemberment.

Such meetings enlarge the white middle term of claim
which quivers between the dramatic red and blue poles
of fight-or-flight.
The claim exercised by pelicans
on the riverbank lawn who tap you for a sandwich
or the water-dragon in flared and fretted display
who opened its head at me, likewise for a sandwich,

by the tiny birds who materialised and sang
when my wife sang in the sleeper-cutting forest
down Stoney Creek Road. And the famous dolphins.
Today, though, men are fighting
the merciful wars of surplus, on the battered river,
making their own wide wings, and water skiers
are hoisting the inherent white banner, making it stretch
and stream both ways at once, like children's drawings
of ships or battle, out in front of the carnival.
A human dream. It barely happens in nature.

The Sleepout

Childhood sleeps in a verandah room
in an iron bed close to the wall
where the winter over the railing
swelled the blind on its timber boom

and splinters picked lint off warm linen
and the stars were out over the hill;
then one wall of the room was forest
and all things in there were to come.

Breathings climbed up on the verandah
when dark cattle rubbed at a corner
and sometimes dim towering rain stood
for forest, and the dry cave hunched woollen.

Inside the forest was lamplit
along tracks to a starry creek bed
and beyond lay the never-fenced country,
its full billabongs all surrounded

by animals and birds, in loud crustings,
and something kept leaping up amongst them.
And out there, to kindle whenever
dark found it, hung the daylight moon.

Louvres

In the banana zone, in the poinciana tropics
reality is stacked on handsbreadth shelving,
open and shut, it is ruled across with lines
as in a gleaming gritty exercise book.

The world is seen through a cranked or levered
weatherboarding of explosive glass
angled floor-to-ceiling. Horizons which metre
the dazzling outdoors into green-edged couplets.

In the louvred latitudes
children fly to sleep in triplanes, and
cool nights are eerie with retracting flaps.

Their houses stand aloft among bougainvillea,
covered bridges that lead down a shining hall
from love to mystery to breakfast,
from babyhood to moving-out day

and visitors shimmer up in columnar gauges
to touch lives lived behind gauze
in a lantern of inventory,
slick vector geometries glossing the months of rain.

There, nudity is dizzily cubist, and directions
have to include: stage left, add an inch of breeze
or: enter a glistening tendril.

Every building of jinked and slatted ledges
is at times a squadron of inside-out
helicopters, humming with rotor fans.

For drinkers under cyclonic pressure, such
a house can be a bridge of scythes –
groundlings scuffing by stop only for dénouements.

But everyone comes out on platforms of command
to survey cloudy flame-trees, the plain of streets, the future:
only then descending to the level of affairs

and if these things are done in the green season
what to do in the crystalline dry? Well
below in the struts of laundry is the four-wheel drive

vehicle in which to make an expedition
to the bush, or as we now say the Land,
the three quarters of our continent
set aside for mystic poetry.

The Edgeless

Floodwater from remote rains has spread out
of the riverine scrub, resuming its mirages.
Mostly shallow, mild water
it ties its hidden drowning strains
taut around old trees, in that low forest
whose skinny shade turns the water taupe. Nests float
and the vaster flat shine is cobbled at wave-shadow points
with little brown melons, just starting to smell rank.

The local station manager, his eyes
still squinting from the greenest green on the place,
the computer screen, strolls out of his office
onto the verandah. Tiny native bees
who fly standing up, like angels, shimmer the garden.
His wife points out their dog Boxer,
pads slipping, tongue slipping out, nails
catching in unseen lurch mineshafts, gamely
teetering along the round top rail of the killing yard.

Where does talk come from? the two ask each other
over teacups. – From the same place as the world.
We have got the word and we don't understand it.
It is like too much. – So we made up a word of our own
as much like nothing else as possible
and gave it to the machines. It made them grow –
And now we can't see the limits of that word either.

Come down off there, Boxer! Who put you up there?

The Drugs of War

On vinegar and sour fish sauce Rome's legions stemmed
    avalanches
of whirling golden warriors whose lands furnished veterans'
    ranches;
when the warriors broke through at last, they'd invented sour
    mash
but they took to sugared wines and failed to hold the lands of
    hash.

By beat of drum in the wars of rum flogged peasant boys faced
    front
and their warrior chiefs conversed coolly, attired for the hunt
and tobacco came in, in a pipe of peace, but joined the pipes of
    war
as an after-smoke of battle, or over the maps before.

All alcohols, all spirits lost strength in the trenches, that belt-fed
     country
then morphine summoned warrior dreams in ruined and would-
     be gentry;
stewed tea and vodka and benzedrine helped quell that mechanized
     fury –
the side that won by half a head then provided judge and jury.

In the acid war the word was Score; rising helicopters cried
     Smack-Smack!
Boys laid a napalm trip on earth and tried to take it back
but the pot boiled over in the rear; fighters tripped on their lines
     of force
and victory went to the supple hard side, eaters of fish sauce.

The perennial war drugs are made in ourselves: sex and adrenalin,
blood, and the endomorphias that transmute defeat and pain
and others hardly less chemical: eagles, justice, loyalty, edge,
the Judas face of every idea, and the fish that ferments in the
     brain.

Letters to the Winner

After the war, and just after marriage and fatherhood
ended in divorce, our neighbour won the special lottery,
an amount then equal to fifteen years of a manager's
salary at the bank, or fifty years' earnings by
a marginal farmer fermenting his clothes in the black
marinade of sweat, up in his mill-logging paddocks.

The district, used to one mailbag, now received two
every mailday. The fat one was for our neighbour.
After a dip or two, he let these bags accumulate
around the plank walls of the kitchen, over the chairs
till on a rainy day, he fed the tail-switching calves,
let the bullocks out of the yard, and pausing at the door
to wash his hands, came inside to read the letters.

Shaken out in a vast mound on the kitchen table
they slid down, slithered to his fingers. *I have 7 children*
I am under the doctor if you could see your way clear
equal Pardners in the Venture God would bless you lovey
assured of our best service for a mere fifteen pounds down
remember you're only lucky I knew you from the paper straightaway

Baksheesh, hissed the pages as he flattened them, baksheesh!
mate if your interested in a fellow diggers problems
old mate a friend in need – the Great Golden Letter
having come, now he was being punished for it.
You sound like a lovely big boy we could have such times
her's my photoe Doll Im wearing my birthday swimsuit
with the right man I would share this infallible system.

When he lifted the stove's iron disc and started feeding in
the pages he'd read, they clutched and streamed up the corrugated
black chimney shaft. And yet he went on reading,
holding each page by its points, feeling an obligation
to read each crude rehearsed lie, each come-on, flat truth,
    extremity:
We might visit you the wise investor a loan a bush man like you

remember we met on Roma Street for your delight and mine
a lick of the sultana – the white moraine kept slipping
its messages to him *you will be accursed* he husked them like cobs
Mr Nouveau Jack old man my legs are all paralysed up.
Black smuts swirled weightless in the room *some good kind person*
like the nausea of a novice free-falling in a deep mine's cage
now I have lost his pension and formed a sticky nimbus round him

but he read on, fascinated by a further human range
not even war had taught him, nor literature glossed for him
since he never read literature. Merely the great reject pile
which high style is there to snub and filter, for readers.
That his one day's reading had a strong taste of what he and war
had made of his marriage is likely; he was not without sympathy

but his leap had hit a wire through which the human is policed.
His head throbbed as if busting with a soundless shout
of immemorial sobbed invective *God-forsaken, God-forsaken*
as he stopped reading, and sat blackened in his riches.

The China Pear Trees

The power of three China pear trees
standing in their splintery timber bark
on an open paddock:

the selector's house that staked and watered them
in Bible times, beside a spaded patch
proved deciduous; it went away in loads,

but after sixty years of standing out,
vanishing in autumn, blizzarding in spring,
among the farmlands' sparse and giant furniture,

after sixty crops gorged on from all directions,
so that no windfalls, fermenting, shrank to lizard-skinned
puree in the short grazed grass,

the trees drew another house, electrified and steaming
but tin-roofed as before for blazing clouds to creak over
and with tiny nude frogs upright again on lamplit glass;

they drew another kitchen garden, and a dam
half scintillating waterlily pleasance, half irrigation,
an ad hoc orchard, Christmas pines, a cud-dropping mower;

they drew a wire fence around acres of enclosure
shaped like a fuel tin, its spout a tunnel of trees
tangled in passionflower and beige-belled wonga vine,

down inside which a floodtime waterfall churns
millet-sized gravel. And they called lush water-leaved trees
like themselves to the stumpholes of gone rainforest

to shade with four seasons the tattered evergreen
oil-haloed face of a subtle fire landscape
(water forest versus fire forest, ancient war of the southern worl

It was this shade in the end, not their coarse bottling fruit
that mirrored the moist creek trees outward, as a culture
containing the old gardener now untying and heaping up

one more summer's stems and chutneys,
his granddaughter walking a horse the colour of her boots
and his tree-shaping son ripping out the odd failed seedling,
"Sorry, tree. I kill and I learn."

The Vol Sprung from Heraldry

Left wing, right wing:
two wings torment our lives,
two wings without a body,
joined, turkey wing and vulture wing

like the badge of an airborne army.
Each has its clients to enfold
and shed lice on. It gets quite underarm
and the other wing lashes at them.

Two wings without a bird –
it is called a *vol* in heraldry –
spinning, fighting, low to the ground,
whomping up evil dusts for our breath.

Sometimes they borrow a head
like the bride-head on a Scots grave,
stone, pitiless in pursed absorption,
drinking blood to digest into thought,

biting out sinews to weave
into an agenda of trap questions.
Only on abstract figures,
statues of the past or future

does it have mercy.
Discarded, it drops from the wings
to burst in the street like a car bomb
– and the lightened, whipping

wings stiffen to a double kinked sword,
left tip up, right point down
in wingovers shedding diseased feathers
and the slashed air bleeds oppression.

Two wings, longing for a body:
left wing, right wing, flexing
still from the noble secret spring
that launched, propels and will exhaust them:

that everything in the end grows boring.

The Megaethon: 1850, 1906-29
i.m. Leo Port

Farmer Cleve, gent., of the Hunter
Valley has ordained that his large
Sydney-built steam engine shall be walked
home under its own power, on iron
shoes serially laid beneath its wheels.
Making four miles a day, it's no fizzer.
He has christened it the Megaethon.

On black iron plates that lean down
and flatten successively, imprinting
rectangular billets of progression
it advances on the Hawkesbury district
hissing, clanking, stoked by freed men.
People run from oat-field and wash-house,
from pot-house and cockpit to gape
at its shackled gait, its belt-drive pulsation:

"Look, Mother, it walks on its knees!" "Aye,
it's praying its way to Wiseman's Ferry,
coughing black smoke out of its steeple!"
Sparks canter by it, cracking whips. Small
native children scream "Buggy-buggy!"
and the iron gangs straighten from their sad
triangular thoughts to watch another
mighty value approach along their spadework.

In that last, dissolving convict year
what passes their wedged grins is a harbinger
not merely of words like *humdinger*, but
of stump-jump ploughs, metal ores made float,
ice plants, keel wings, a widening vote,
the world's harvesters, the utility truck, rotary
engines pipemoulds lawnmowers – this motor the
slaves watch strikes a ringing New World note.

As, tilting, stayed with ropes and pulleys,
the Megaethon descends a plateau edge,
casting shoes, crushing sandstone, only
the poorest, though, watching from dry bush
in that chain-tugging year, last before the gold rush,
know that here is a centre of the world
and that one who can rattle the inverted
cosmos is stamping to her stamping ground.

Not guided by such truth, the Megaethon
veers towards rum-and-opium stops,
waits, cooling, beside a slab bordello
and leans at last in upland swamp,

flat-footed, becoming salvage,
freight for ribald bullockies. Its polygonal
rhythms will engender no balladry;
it won't break the trench-lines at Vicksburg.

The engine goes home to make chaff
and the idea of the Megaethon
must travel underground. Stockmen gallop
above it. It travels underground.
Secret ballots and boxkites are invented,
unions form, national purposes gather
above it. It travels underground;
for fifty years it travels underground

losing its first name. It surfaces
in Melbourne at last, in the mind
of one Frank Bottrill, who calls
his wheel of three sliding plates
the Pedrail or Dreadnought wheel
"for travelling across country in all
conditions, where roads may be absent."
In all but name, the Megaethon

is abroad again, now clearing country,
now ploughing the new farms. Its jointed
wheel-plates go to war on artillery
lashing back the Ottoman Empire
from Suez to Damascus. The monster
guns of Flanders advance and recoil
on many-slatted wheels. Tanks grind by them,
collateral descendants of the Megaethon

which itself remains in innocent
rebirth in its own hemisphere.
Its largest example, Big Lizzie
spends the mid-war years crossing Victoria
and following the Murray through Gunbower,
Mystic Park and Day Trap to Mildura.
From its deck eighteen feet above ground
crews wave to the river paddlesteamers:

"Gutter sailors! Our ship don't *need* water!"
Submarine in the mallee forests
Big Lizzie leaves a shattered wake;
she wades marsh, crosses grass fires' negative
landscape: black ground, bleached rattling trees;
her slamming gait shuts the earth down
but her following ploughs reopen it
in long rising loaves. Soldiers follow her

and turn into farmers sewing full
wheat bags with a large darning needle.
Giant workhorse born between the ages
of plodding feet and highway speeds
it takes lorries a decade to catch
and relegate Lizzie's oil-engined shuffle.
The Megaethon thus re-enters a quaintness
at two miles an hour, having,

though ponderous, only lightly existed
(twice so far) and never directly
shed blood. And there, repaired with wire
from strict fences, it still walks the trackless,
slow as workaday, available for metaphor,
laying down and picking up the squeezed-
fragrant iron suit-cards of its patience,
crews making mugs of tea from its boiler.

Fastness

I am listening for words the eldest
of three brothers must have uttered
magically, out of their whole being

to make a sergeant major look down
at the stamped grass, and not have them stopped
as they walked, not trooped, off his shouting

143

showground parade, in the brown
fatal clothes and pink boots they'd been given,

to retrieve their own horses and vanish
bearing even the unloaded strap rifles
the Government would still be pursuing
a decade later, along with the brothers.

I have come as far as officials
and sergeants ever came, telling their
hillbilly yarns: the boy-headed calf,
the barbed wire across the teenage bedroom,
the dead wife backpacked forty miles
in a chaff bag, but gutted to save weight.
I have passed where their cars' spoke wheels
slid and stopped, and the silent vines hung.

Since beyond the exact words, I need
the gesture with which they were said,
the horizons and hill air that shaped them,
the adze-faceted timbers of the kitchen
where they were repeated to the old people

who, having heard nothing about war,
had sent the boys three days round trip
in to town for saltpetre and tobacco.
I need the angle of cloud forest
visible through that door, the fire chains
and the leaf tastes of tank water there.

I will only have history, lacking these,
not the words as they have to be
spoken out, in such moments:

centrally, so as to pass the mind
of cheerful blustering authority
and paralyse it in its dream –

right in the unmeant nick of time
even as the rails were shutting
on the wide whooping yard of adventure
and making it a cattle chute
that led through jokes and accoutrements
to the long blood trail a-winding.

I need not think the brothers were
unattracted by a world venture
in aid of the woman Belgium
or not drawn by herd-warmth towards
the glorious manhunting promised them
by fellows round pipe-drawing fires
outside the beast-pavilions they slept in.

I need remember only the angel
poverty wrestles with in vast places
to know the power of abandon
people want, with control, to touch
when they tell hillbilly stories

and knowing it well, to uncover
how the brothers missed their legendary
Anzac chance, I need only
sit on this rusty bedstead, on a known
vanished sleepout verandah and reflect

how the lifelong lordly of space
might speak, in discernment of spirits
at the loud surcingled slave-master's
very first bawled genial insult
to any of theirs. Not the camel's-back-
breaking, trapped slight, but the first.

1980 in a Street of Federation Houses

In 1980, in a street of Federation houses
a man is brushing his hair inside a car
while waiting for his children. It is his access day.

Men down the street – one perched high
as an oldtime sailor, others hauling long lines –
are dismantling a tree, from the top down. A heavy
branch drops, out of keen gristing noise, and runs
dragging all the stumpy hauliers
inwards on their ropes, then hangs swinging.

In 1964, the same man, slightly plumper
is proclaiming in the Union bar *Now let
us watch the angels dance on the head of a pill!*
He does not mean, but swallows, a methedrine tablet.

In the same year he consents for the first time
to find the woodchoppers at the Easter Show
faintly comical, in their cricketing whites and singlets,

starting in handicap order to knock on wood:
one chopper, two choppier, then a clobbering
increment of cobbers down in the grunting arena –

he assigns them to 1955, an obsolete year
and the whole Labour Movement
shifts and re-levels in his mind
like mercury, needing new calibrations.

In 1824 in another country
present to his albums, small children run all day
breathing lint in a cavernous tropic factory
lit by weak globes on which older lint has caramelled.

They work from dawn to palm-frond-clattering dark
loading bales of packaged shirts on to trucks
driven by tribesmen who smoke, as they do themselves,
like the Industrial Revolution, paper chimneys in their cursing
    mouths.

Upcountry, men of the Thirties in 1950s uniform
instruct youths and girls of the starving fourteen hundreds
how to conjure with rifles the year Seventeen Ninety-two.
Their ammunition is the first packaged goods they have handled.

To reproduce yourself is to admit defeat!
His dashing friend had said it, in the year
he was told about cadmium fish, and blamed for the future.
To reproduce oneself? Who ever did that?

Most, perhaps, before the Industrial Revolution
but then permanent death came in; all the years,
all the centuries now had to fit into one lifetime.

As did heaven. Which drew hell.
The Bomb and the Club Méditerranée had to lie
down together –. He begins to see his educators
as missionaries of the new unending death.

He shifts to another year, along the band
of his car's stereo, and his children are playing
in a tent on sandy grass;
can there be a time in which this scene is not a bibelot?

Now that up the suburban street that leads to the past
a figure is leading not greyhounds but Afghan hounds
and on the beach beyond, women who enter the surf
shielding a web of dusty lint emerge
and each is wearing a feather!

The Milk Lorry

Now the milk lorry is a polished submarine
that rolls up at midday, attaches a trunk and inhales
the dairy's tank to a frosty snore in minutes

but its forerunner was the high-tyred barn of crisp mornings,
reeking Diesel and mammary, hazy in its roped interior
as a carpet under beaters, as it crashed along potholed lanes

cooeeing at schoolgirls. Long planks like unshipped oars
butted, levelling in there, because between each farm's
stranded wharf of milk cans, the work was feverish slotting

of floors above floors, for load. It was sling out the bashed
paint-collared empties and waltz in the full,
stumbling on their rims under ribaldry, tilting their big gallons

then the schoolboy's calisthenic, hoisting steel men man-high
till the glancing hold was a magazine of casque armour,
a tinplate tween-decks, a seminar engrossed

in one swaying tradition, behind the speeding doorways
that tempted a truant to brace and drop, short of town
and spend the day, with book or not, down under

the bridge of a river that by dinnertime would be
tongueing like cattledogs, or down a moth-dusty reach
where the fish-feeding milk boat and cedar barge once floated.

The Butter Factory

It was built of things that must not mix:
paint, cream and water, fire and dusty oil.
You heard the water dreaming in its large
kneed pipes, up from the weir. And the cordwood
our fathers cut for the furnace stood in walls
like the sleeper-stacks of a continental railway.

The cream arrived in lorried tides; its procession
crossed a platform of workers' stagecraft: *Come here
Friday-Legs! Or I'll feel your hernia* –
Overalled in milk's colour, men moved the heart of milk,

148

separated into thousands, along a roller track – *Trucks?*
That one of mine, son, it pulls like a sixteen-year-old –
to the tester who broached the can lids, causing fat tears,
who tasted, dipped and did his thin stoppered chemistry
on our labour, as the empties chattered downstage and fumed.

Under the high roof, black-crusted and stainless steels
were walled apart: black romped with leather belts
but paddlewheels sailed the silvery vats where muscles
of the one deep cream were exercised to a bullion
to be blocked in paper. And between waves of delivery
the men trod on water, hosing the rainbows of a shift.

It was damp April even at Christmas round every
margin of the factory. Also it opened the mouth
to see tackles on glibbed gravel, and the mossed char louvres
of the ice-plant's timber tower streaming with
heavy rain all day, above the droughty paddocks
of the totem cows round whom our lives were dancing.

Bats' Ultrasound

Sleeping-bagged in a duplex wing
with fleas, in rock-cleft or building
radar bats are darkness in miniature,
their whole face one tufty crinkled ear
with weak eyes, fine teeth bared to sing.

Few are vampires. None flit through the mirror.
Where they flutter at evening's a queer
tonal hunting zone above highest C.
Insect prey at the peak of our hearing
drone re to their detailing tee:

ah, eyrie-ire; aero hour, eh?
O'er our ur-area (our era aye
ere your raw row) we air our array,
err, yaw, row wry – aura our orrery,
our eerie ü our ray, our arrow.

A rare ear, our aery Yahweh.

Roman Cage-cups

Excavate, at a constant curving interval
a layer of air between the inner and outer
skins of a glass beaker, leaving only odd struts integral;

at the same time, at the same ablative atom-
by-atom rate, sculpt the outer shell to an openwork
of rings, or foliage, or a muscular Elysium –

It made for calm paste and a steady file
that one false stroke, one twitch could cost a year's time,
a good billet, your concubine. Only the cups were held noble.

Plebs and immigrants fashioned them, punters
who ate tavern-fried pike and talked Vulgate.
The very first might have been made as a stunt, as

the life-gambit of a slave. Or a joke on the feasting scene:
a wine-bowl no one coarsely drunk could handle
nor, since baseless, easily put down,

a marvel of undercutting, a glass vessel
so costly it would exact that Roman gravity,
draw blood, and feud, if grasped without suavity.

The one depicting Thracian Lycurgus
strangled by amorous vines for slighting Bacchus
could hardly have survived an old-time bacchanal.

150

Where polish is cutting and festivity an ice
and most meaning paradox, it is an age of cool.
Culture has lifted off and impends above us

on brittle legs, always more or less transparent.
Splendour of social vertigo. Even to describe it serves its luxury.
But this is the fourth, that is, the eleventh century:

war-chiefs are coming whose descendants in turn
will learn to exalt, to suspend the new fraternal
faith that triumphed lately. So the engravers groove on

under the fixed heavens, into that driest liquid,
miming a low but vast space, never roofed entirely –
as between the idea and its word, a global interstice.

The glass flowers of Harvard, monks' micro pen-lace, a
        chromosome
needled to grow wings on a horse (which they'd also have done),
the freely moving ivory dragons-inside-a-dragon

ball of Cathay – the impossible is a groove:
why else do we do it? Even some given a choice
would rather work the metaphors than live them, in society.

But nothing, since sparkle became permanent in the thumbs
and rib-cages of these craftsmen, has matched their handiwork
for gentleness, or edge. They put the gape into agapé,

these factory products, of all Rome's underground Gothic:
cups transfigured by hand, too delicate to break.
Some, exported beyond the Rhine as a *miss-*

ion civilisatrice, have survived complete and unchipped
a sesquimillennium longer than the trumpets (allude,
allude) of the arena. Rome's very hardest rock.